MACAT

An Analysis of

Mahbub ul Haq's

Reflections on Human Development

Riley Quinn

CONTENTS

THE MACAT LIBRARY

The Macat Library is a series of unique academic explorations of seminal works in the humanities and social sciences – books and papers that have had a significant and widely recognised impact on their disciplines. It has been created to serve as much more than just a summary of what lies between the covers of a great book. It illuminates and explores the influences on, ideas of, and impact of that book. Our goal is to offer a learning resource that encourages critical thinking and fosters a better, deeper understanding of important ideas.

Each publication is divided into three Sections: Influences, Ideas, and Impact. Each Section has four Modules. These explore every important facet of the work, and the responses to it.

This Section-Module structure makes a Macat Library book easy to use, but it has another important feature. Because each Macat book is written to the same format, it is possible (and encouraged!) to cross-reference multiple Macat books along the same lines of inquiry or research. This allows the reader to open up interesting interdisciplinary pathways.

To further aid your reading, lists of glossary terms and people mentioned are included at the end of this book (these are indicated by an asterisk [*] throughout) – as well as a list of works cited.

Macat has worked with the University of Cambridge to identify the elements of critical thinking and understand the ways in which six different skills combine to enable effective thinking.
Three allow us to fully understand a problem; three more give us the tools to solve it. Together, these six skills make up the **PACIER** model of critical thinking. They are:

ANALYSIS – understanding how an argument is built
EVALUATION – exploring the strengths and weaknesses of an argument
INTERPRETATION – understanding issues of meaning

CREATIVE THINKING – coming up with new ideas and fresh connections
PROBLEM-SOLVING – producing strong solutions
REASONING – creating strong arguments

To find out more, visit **WWW.MACAT.COM.**

CRITICAL THINKING AND *REFLECTIONS ON HUMAN DEVELOPMENT*

Primary critical thinking skill: REASONING
Secondary critical thinking skill: EVALUATION

What is the ultimate goal of any human society? There have been many answers to this question. But by producing a series of notably well-structured arguments, economist Mahbub ul Haq's *Reflections on Human Development* persuaded readers that the goal should be defined quite simply as the requirement that each society improve the lives of its citizens.

If this is the agreed aim, Haq continues, then economic development should be designed to support human development. His well-structured reasoning helped development economists recalibrate much of what had previously been regarded as self-evident; that economic productivity was the main barometer of social well being. The work had a profound effect, and Haq's thinking helped produce a new understanding of what 'development' actually meant.

Haq conscientiously mapped out arguments and counter-arguments to persuade readers that development did not simply mean an increase in productivity, but rather an increase in human development – the capability of people to live the lives they want to. By bringing the abstract back to the concrete, Haq reevaluated the neoliberal reasoning that suggested economic development necessarily benefitted everybody. And, by virtue of his strong command of reasoning, Haq showed how economic development provided no guarantees that rich people would spend money on improving health, education or other human development outcomes for the poor.

ABOUT THE AUTHOR OF THE ORIGINAL WORK

Born in 1934, **Mahbub ul Haq** was a Pakistani economist who studied in both the United Kingdom and the United States. After working at the World Bank, and then at the highest levels of planning in his native Pakistan, Haq joined the United Nations. In 1990 he introduced a radical new way of measuring development as part of his work at the United Nations Development Programme. Rather than looking at economic growth alone, his Human Development Index (HDI) measured not only a country's average income earned per person, but also life expectancy and literacy levels. The HDI showed Haq's desire to harness growth to social improvement. By the time he died in 1998, Haq's visionary thinking on development had become accepted as mainstream policy.

ABOUT THE AUTHOR OF THE ANALYSIS

Riley Quinn holds master's degrees in politics and international relations from both LSE and the University of Oxford.

ABOUT MACAT

GREAT WORKS FOR CRITICAL THINKING

Macat is focused on making the ideas of the world's great thinkers accessible and comprehensible to everybody, everywhere, in ways that promote the development of enhanced critical thinking skills.

It works with leading academics from the world's top universities to produce new analyses that focus on the ideas and the impact of the most influential works ever written across a wide variety of academic disciplines. Each of the works that sit at the heart of its growing library is an enduring example of great thinking. But by setting them in context – and looking at the influences that shaped their authors, as well as the responses they provoked – Macat encourages readers to look at these classics and game-changers with fresh eyes. Readers learn to think, engage and challenge their ideas, rather than simply accepting them.

'Macat offers an amazing first-of-its-kind tool for interdisciplinary learning and research. Its focus on works that transformed their disciplines and its rigorous approach, drawing on the world's leading experts and educational institutions, opens up a world-class education to anyone.'

Andreas Schleicher
Director for Education and Skills, Organisation for Economic
Co-operation and Development

'Macat is taking on some of the major challenges in university education … They have drawn together a strong team of active academics who are producing teaching materials that are novel in the breadth of their approach.'

Prof Lord Broers,
former Vice-Chancellor of the University of Cambridge

'The Macat vision is exceptionally exciting. It focuses upon new modes of learning which analyse and explain seminal texts which have profoundly influenced world thinking and so social and economic development. It promotes the kind of critical thinking which is essential for any society and economy. This is the learning of the future.'

Rt Hon Charles Clarke, former UK Secretary of State for Education

'The Macat analyses provide immediate access to the critical conversation surrounding the books that have shaped their respective discipline, which will make them an invaluable resource to all of those, students and teachers, working in the field.'

Professor William Tronzo, University of California at San Diego

WAYS IN TO THE TEXT

KEY POINTS

- Mahbub ul Haq (1934–98) was a Pakistani economist who worked for the global intergovernmental body the United Nations.*

- Haq's book *Reflections on Human Development* describes the "human development"* revolution, in which the focus of development changed from raising the economic productivity of the world's nations to directly improving people's lives.

- Human development was fundamental in formulating the UN's Millennium Development Goals*—targets for gender equality, environmental sustainability, the eradication of poverty and hunger, and so on.

Who Was Mahbub ul Haq?

Mahbub ul Haq, the author of *Reflections on Human Development*, was born in 1934 in the Punjab, then British India, a region of what is today Pakistan. After taking a degree in economics at the University of Punjab, he moved to the United Kingdom and gained a second undergraduate degree in economics at the University of Cambridge. It was there that he befriended the Nobel Prize-winning Indian economist Amartya Sen.* This friendship was to be profoundly influential for both. Haq completed his studies at Yale University before accepting an academic post at Harvard University.

Haq did not, however, remain in academia. Instead, he returned to Pakistan, where he became the chief economist of Pakistan's Planning Commission—the governmental body dealing with finance, public policy, and development— in the 1960s. He promoted free-market reforms around the country as a route to prosperity for the Pakistani people. But his hopes were not met; instead of wealth trickling down throughout Pakistani society, the benefits of economic growth were concentrated in the hands of an elite, as 22 prominent families enjoyed 66 percent of Pakistan's economic expansion.

Disappointed, Haq left Pakistan to work as the director of policy planning at the World Bank*—an international financial institution based in the US city of Washington that provides loans to low-income countries. After moving between Pakistan and America, in 1989 he took up a role with the United Nations Development Program* in New York. Working with Sen and a group of world-leading economists, Haq inaugurated the United Nations Development Program (UNDP)'s *Human Development Report** in 1990. This landmark publication changed the way people thought about economics. Instead of focusing exclusively on economic growth, Haq and his colleagues argued that development should focus on improving the lives of real people. The *Report* has been published annually ever since.

Haq died in 1998. He was 64.

What Does *Reflections* Say?

Reflections on Human Development, published in 1995, summarizes Mahbub ul Haq's work with the United Nations Development Program (UNDP). Haq joined the United Nations in 1989 and played a pivotal role in changing people's understanding of the term "development." In the 1980s "development" was understood to mean "economic growth" and "an increase in productivity." Haq, however, understood "development" to mean "human development." His ideas were influenced by the economist Amartya Sen, who believed that the goal of politics and economics should be to increase our capability to live the lives we desire to lead. Applying this theory to the practical work of development, Haq argued that human development should be measured. Following this, economic resources could be targeted toward institutions that helped to support people's quality of life.

The idea of human development is based on a number of core premises. First, society exists to give people the best lives possible. Second, to attain the best life possible, people must decide what they want to do and be, and then pursue those goals. Economic development should enable them to do so.

This does not initially seem a controversial idea. But how can it be achieved? Haq's thinking becomes revolutionary when he rejects the idea that economic development alone will lead to human development; on the contrary, he argues, economic development can favor the wealthy and well connected and still exclude the poor from prosperity. There is no guarantee that the rich will spend money on improving health and education outcomes for the poor.

This idea ran counter to the dominant development ideology at the time, neoliberalism.* According to neoliberal thought, free markets and minimal government interference will motivate people to start businesses and earn money. Haq disagrees. He argues that if society exists for the improvement of the lives of its citizens, economic growth should also be turned toward this purpose; it is an absurd situation if greater prosperity leads to greater inequality, and people are worse off.

Haq's main concern was to refocus development towards human goals. To do this, he created the Human Development Index* (HDI)—arguably the most important invention of Haq's new approach. It combined indicators in economic prosperity, educational attainment, and longevity (life expectancy) to produce a more detailed, integrated, and complete picture of a country's development. If we have a new way to look at how well countries are doing, we also need to understand how they fall behind. For example, Haq says that military spending is a waste of resources. He calls for resources to be diverted from the military and given to improving people's lives.

The Human Development Index was introduced in the first *Human Development Report* (1990), now an annual UN publication. It was a landmark moment. Development was being assessed in a wholly new way.

Over the following years, as Haq's ideas were accepted as mainstream, they led to the creation of the United Nation's Millennium Development Goals: eight internationally approved development aspirations, which included eradicating hunger, achieving universal primary education, and promoting gender equality. The book *Reflections* explores how Haq's ideas went from being regarded as revolutionary to becoming established wisdom.

Why Does *Reflections* Matter?

Reflections, and the *Human Development Reports* upon which it is based, are important because they are the works in which Mahbub ul Haq champions the idea that development should focus on benefitting people, rather than on simple economic growth. This transformation in thinking was instrumental in creating the UN Millennium Development Goals (MDGs). The aim was to achieve these eight global targets by 2015:

* Eradicate hunger and extreme poverty
* Achieve universal primary education
* Promote gender equality and empower women
* Reduce child mortality
* Improve maternal health
* Combat HIV/AIDS, malaria, and other diseases
* Ensure environmental sustainability
* Develop a global partnership for development.

The MDGs were certainly ambitious: they aimed to halve the number of people living in extreme poverty. Their goal of making life better for the very worst off contrasts significantly with the more "technical" view of development taken in the past. Post-2015, the goals have been reformulated. The new goals emphasize environmental issues and girls' education.

After 1990 some states began to produce their own *Human Development Report*. This was a vision of economic growth that both donor countries and recipient countries could buy into. Over the years the Human Development Index has been refined to add measurements of gender equality, political freedom, and human rights. Haq's work had broadened the focus of development and made "human development" a standard approach. Even the institutions Haq once criticized, such as the World Bank and the International Monetary Fund* (an organization that aims to foster monetary cooperation, financial stability, high employment, and economic growth through the administration of loans), have gone on to adopt his ideas.

Studying the human development revolution can help readers in a number of ways. First, it helps us think about what it really means to be part of the global poor. It prompts us to consider how easy it is to take basic capabilities, such as being healthy and educated, for granted, and to consider just how important these capabilities are in the journey to prosperity. The idea that development should work to enlarge the freedom of citizens in the developing world may seem obvious today, but when Haq was writing *Reflections* this was not the consensus.

Second, *Reflections* discusses how an intellectual revolution can take place, describing how the widely held presumption that economic growth is linked to social progress was discarded. This, however, prompts the question of whether discarding this presumption was correct. Thinking about Haq's work also prompts readers to pose another important question: where do the *economics* of development end, and the *politics* begin?

SECTION 1
INFLUENCES

MODULE 1
THE AUTHOR AND THE
HISTORICAL CONTEXT

KEY POINTS

- *Reflections on Human Development* reveals a landmark shift in development thinking, from concern with economic productivity to a concern with improving people's lives.

- Mahbub ul Haq worked in Pakistan's Planning Commission and served as Special Advisor to the United Nations Development Program (UNDP)*—a body dedicated to reducing poverty and to a number of broader human development* goals including promoting global health, literacy, and democracy.

- When the Cold War* ended in 1991, development policy (the official stance and method of donor states or organizations on how and where to disperse funds intended for development) was extended to many more countries. But it also became clear that the existing models of development policy were achieving disappointing results.

Why Read This Text?

Mahbub ul Haq's *Reflections on Human Development* (1995) lays out Haq's reflections about how to measure development. While the term "development" had historically referred to economic growth, Haq argues that *human* development should be at the heart of development planning and policy. He believes that the purpose of development is not to maximize the wealth of a state, but to maximize the choices available to the citizens of that state.

> ❝ Few ideas in development policy have, in recent times, captured the imagination of economists, policy makers, political activists, and aid agencies, as much as the *Human Development Reports*, written by a team led by Mahbub ul Haq and published annually since 1990 by the United Nations Development Program. ❞
>
> Sanjaya Baru, "Mahbub ul Haq and Human Development"

This human development model starts with a seemingly simple modification to orthodox neoliberal* development theory. The neoliberal approach to development seeks to maximize the *quantity* of a state's growth by maximizing its Gross Domestic Product (GDP)*—the market value of all goods and services produced within a given state in a year. In contrast, Haq's human development model seeks to maximize the *quantity* and the *quality* of a state's growth. "Quality," for Haq, means that development should be concerned with a fair distribution of wealth, sustainability, productivity, and empowerment.[1] Growth, he argues, should be maximized and distributed as much as possible.

Reflections grew out of Haq's work for the United Nations Development Program (UNDP). This executive board was set up in 1965 and is dedicated to reducing poverty and to the promotion of issues such as global health, literacy, and democracy.

Part of Haq's role was to oversee the UNDP's annual *Human Development Report*.* These reports, written by a team of leading scholars, economists, and statespeople, assess a wide range of human development indicators. Haq was responsible for the first six reports, published between 1990 and 1996. In *Reflections*, rather than advancing new ideas, he summarizes this work and the new way of thinking that it embodies. He calls for further progress to be made in human development.

Author's Life

The Pakistani economist Mahbub ul Haq was born to a Muslim family in 1934, in the Punjab region of the Indian subcontinent before it was partitioned* into India and Pakistan; he was educated in economics at the University of Punjab, but continued his education at the University of Cambridge, where he took another undergraduate degree in economics. It was at Cambridge that he met the economist and philosopher Amartya Sen,* who became a close friend and professional associate. Haq pursued graduate work at Yale University, earning his doctorate before accepting a post-doctoral position at Harvard University. Following this he returned to Pakistan, where he took up a government position as chief economist of Pakistan's Planning Commission—a governmental body dealing with finance, public policy, and development.[2]

This work in Pakistan was followed by a stint at the World Bank* in Washington between 1972 and 1982. Haq then returned to Pakistan for a further six years, before joining the UNDP in New York in 1988. The UNDP's first official *Human Development Report* was produced in 1990. Haq's involvement influenced *Reflections* profoundly. He played a key role in pushing the UN to produce these reports and to extend this work through the 1990s.

The first report represented a devastating criticism of neoliberal development orthodoxy with its emphasis on free markets. The report's content and methodology was created by Haq and his colleagues, while its core ideas were influenced by Sen, who believed that the state should exist to help its citizens flourish. The book is shot through with United Nations concerns. It is notable for its optimism in calling for more states to pay attention to the UN and reorganize their own development strategies.

Author's Background

The end of the Cold War in the early 1990s—a long, tense, nuclear stand-off between the Soviet Union* and its allies and the United

States and its allies—opened up many formerly communist states to the political and economic resources of the West. Haq argued this would raise "new aspirations for people-centered development models."[3] Old models no longer sufficed: the world was ready for a new way of looking at development.

In 1986 the former managing director of the International Monetary Fund (IMF)* Jacques de Larosière* said "adjustment that pays attention to the health, nutritional, and educational requirements of the most vulnerable groups is going to protect the human condition better than adjustment that ignores them."[4] Much has been made of the term "adjustment,"* but this term really refers to economic modernization: creating globally integrated, efficient, free-market economies. "This means, in turn," Larosière continued, "that the authorities have to be concerned not only with whether they close the fiscal deficit but also how they do so."[5]

The neoliberal approach had begun to appear unsatisfactory; as Haq argues: "The human costs of Structural Adjustment Programs* undertaken in many development countries under the aegis of the IMF and the World Bank had been extremely harsh."[6] These "structural adjustment packages" were neoliberal market-oriented economic reforms that the IMF and the World Bank, two influential financial institutions, required "development countries" to implement if they were to receive the loans they needed; in short, states were being modernized without regard to preserving the well-being of their citizens. Growth, which aimed to maximize any given country's overall gross income, was prioritized. In Haq's view, these packages made it acceptable for living standards to fall and for inequality to rise.

Haq's work with the Planning Commission in Pakistan had shown him the real effects of the neoliberal approach. Pakistan enjoyed significant growth—"per capita* income grew at an average of 3.6 percent per year ... manufacturing grew at more than 10 percent per year."[7] But, Haq writes: "It was evident that most of the population had remained virtually untouched by the forces of economic change."[8] In fact, 66 percent of this impressive growth was going to just 22 prominent families. This realization led to Haq's groundbreaking United Nations *Human Development Report*, which aimed to present a viable, equitable alternative to neoliberal growth approaches.

NOTES

1   Mahbub ul Haq, *Reflections on Human Development* (Oxford: Oxford University Press, 1995), 16.

2   Amartya Sen and Tam Dalyell, "Obituary: Mahbub ul Haq," *Independent*, August 3, 1998, accessed October 21, 2015, http://www.independent. co.uk/arts-entertainment/obituary-mahbub-ul Haq-1169323.html.

3   Haq, *Reflections*, 25.

4   Quoted in James P. Grant, "Introduction," *UNICEF Annual Report 1987*, 4, accessed October 21, 2015, http://www.unicef.org/about/history/files/ unicef_annual_report_1987.pdf.

5   Quoted in Grant, "Introduction," 4.

6   Haq, *Reflections*, 25.

7   M. S. Jillani and Masooda Bano, "From 'Growth' to 'Growth With a Social Conscience,'" in *Pioneering the Human Development Revolution: An Intellectual Biography of Mahbub ul Haq*, eds. Khadija Haq and Richard Ponzio (Oxford: Oxford University Press, 2008), 18–22.

8   Mahbub ul Haq, *The Poverty Curtain: Choices for the Third World* (New York: Columbia University Press, 1976), 6.

MODULE 2
ACADEMIC CONTEXT

KEY POINTS

- The field of study in which *Reflections on Human Development* engages—political economy*—is concerned with the ways economic and political forces interact.
- The ancient Greek philosopher Aristotle* opened the field with his inquiry into what happiness is, and what sorts of societies produce it; further refinement through liberal* thinkers emphasized freedom and economic growth.
- Haq believed governments ought to engage in redistribution to ensure that economic growth was accompanied by increasing freedom.

The Work in its Context

Mahbub ul Haq's *Reflections on Human Development* is a work of political economy. This field is concerned with how social and political institutions interact with economic forces to produce different outcomes. Political economy is a balance between moral philosophy—philosophical inquiry into ethics—and technical knowledge. This could be summed up as "practical wisdom": political economists have to work out the "why" and the "how," meaning they have to deduce why something is good, and how that good is to be achieved. This concept is called *phronesis*, a Greek word for intelligent, practical thought.

In his *Nicomachean Ethics*, the fourth-century B.C.E. philosopher Aristotle laid out the concept of *phronesis* as a guide to help people create just laws. Aristotle believed that legislation underpins just societies; *phronesis* helps people to define and therefore attain a just society.[1]

> ❝ Every state is a community of some kind, and every community is established with a view to some good; for mankind will always act in order to obtain that which they think good. ❞
> Aristotle, *Politics*

Haq's work is located in this long tradition of political and social theory. His belief that societies should be valued "by the extent to which they promote the human good" points to Aristotle.[2] Aristotle argues that a society is formed initially to tend to the "bare needs of life": food, shelter, and defense.[3] However, it quickly turns to a higher purpose—existing not for the sake of "mere life," but "for the sake of the good life."[4] For Aristotle, the "good life" is the virtuous life—the life lived well, justly, and for the higher purpose of "excellence."[5] Society, therefore, exists to raise those who live in it up to new heights of excellence—that is, human flourishing.*

Aristotle's argument that "wealth is evidently not the good we are seeking, for it is merely useful and for the sake of something else," was particularly important to Haq.[6] It is not enough for society to support people's lives—it should improve them. This is the distinction between maximizing prosperity, and maximizing "good living."

Overview of the Field

More than 2,000 years after Aristotle, the eighteenth-century German philosopher Immanuel Kant* introduced another concept that would influence Haq. In his *Groundwork of the Metaphysics of Morals* (1785), Kant presented a defense of human equality. Kant defines a universal principle: a principle that applies to all people, which can be reasonably agreed to by all people, and can be applied universally at all times. This "categorical imperative" (or unconditional moral law) is that all humans must be treated "as end and never merely as means."[7] People, in other words, must be respected equally, as their lives are all directed by their own reasoned motivations. "For rational beings," Kant wrote, "all stand under the law that every one of them ought to treat itself and all others never merely as means, but always at the same time as [an] end in itself."[8] Therefore it is not permissible to discount the reasoned motivations of one person in order to achieve one's own reasoned motivations.

Kant provided the principle of equality. The Scottish moral philosopher Adam Smith* then applied that principle to economics. In his book *The Wealth of Nations* (1776), Smith notes that the economic and social system of capitalism* based on the division of labor (the specialization of tasks in industrial production) is mostly good for increasing the overall wealth of a society. But he also suggests that this increase in efficiency may have social costs: the laborer's "dexterity at his own particular trade seems, in this manner, to be acquired at the expense of his intellectual, social, and martial virtues," and the laboring poor will inevitably fall into this state—that is, of living a lesser life—"unless the government takes some pains to prevent it."[9]

Academic Influences

Kant and Smith provide some basic tenets of liberalism:* equality and the social effects of economic growth. These ideas help us to understand the most important economic debate of the twentieth century. This was the debate between followers of Keynesian economics,* according to which governments both could and should intervene in the economy, and those of Austrian economics,* which holds that governments should intervene as little as possible—if it all.

In his book *The General Theory of Employment, Interest, and Money* (1936) the British economist John Maynard Keynes* argues that governments should intervene in the economy in order to promote full employment. Keynes says that the government could tax, spend, and redistribute resources in order to stimulate the economy to employ everyone. At the very core of the theory was the idea that government spending, especially on the poor, created more spending overall, and therefore caused the economy to grow. For Keynes the *distribution* of wealth, as well as its overall level, mattered.[10]

In contrast, the Austrian British economist Friedrich Hayek* of the Austrian school of economics believes in the power of markets to allocate resources efficiently. He says they did this through the price signal: when a commodity is in demand, the price rises, and more is made until the price drops. In that way everyone gets what they want. Hayek argues that when the economy is allowed to run without interference, prosperity will "trickle down"* from those who benefit the most from the system, and become wealthiest, to the state's poorest.

Hayek believes that if governments try to allocate resources efficiently they would fail to satisfy everyone. More, a government that overly concerned itself with the distribution of wealth (that is, taxation and planning) would pose a grave threat to individual liberty. If that were to happen, Hayek says, the "state ceases to be a piece of utilitarian machinery." Instead, it "imposes on its members its views on all moral questions, whether these views be moral or highly immoral."[11]

NOTES

1   Aristotle, *Nicomachean Ethics*, trans. C. D. C. Reeve (Indianapolis: Hackett, 2014), 105, book VI, chapter 8, 11142^a/23–5.

2   Mahbub ul Haq, *Reflections on Human Development* (New Delhi: Oxford University Press India, 1999), 13.

3   Aristotle, *The Politics and the Constitution of Athens*, ed. Stephen Everson (Cambridge: Cambridge University Press, 1996), 12, book I, chapter 1, 1252^b/30.

4   Aristotle, *The Politics*, 12, book I, chapter 1, 1252^b/31.

5   Aristotle, *The Politics*, 80, book III, chapter 12, 1282^a/39–40.

6   Haq, *Reflections*, 13.

7   Immanuel Kant, *Groundwork for the Metaphysics of Morals*, trans. Allen W. Wood (New Haven: Yale University Press, 2002), 47.

8   Kant, *Groundwork,* 51.

9   Adam Smith, *An Enquiry into the Nature and Causes of the Wealth of Nations* (New York: Random House, 1937), 734–5.

10   John Maynard Keynes, *The General Theory of Employment, Interest, and Money* (London: Macmillan, 1954), 372–3.

11   F. A. Hayek, *The Road to Serfdom: Texts and Documents – the Definitive Edition*, ed. Bruce Caldwell (Chicago: Chicago University Press, 2008),115.

MODULE 3
THE PROBLEM

KEY POINTS

- When Haq was writing, the main question that drove development policy was how to prompt economic growth in underdeveloped states.

- The orthodox position was that income growth through reforms that favored the market was the most effective route to prosperity.

- Haq, and Amartya Sen,* argued that poverty was multidimensional (that is, one can lack in many respects, not just income. For example, if one has money but no education, one's life chances can remain limited).

Core Question

The core question in Mahbub ul Haq's *Reflections on Human Development* is the same as that of the Indian American economist Debraj Ray's* book *Development Economics* (1998): the issue of how to "raise the income, well-being, and economic capabilities of peoples everywhere."[1]

One of the most obvious ways to achieve this is to raise the income of the state itself; in theory, wealth will naturally "trickle down"* as the state's overall income rises. Through the 1980s, however, it became obvious to Haq that in several countries "human lives were shriveling even as economic production was expanding."[2] The goal of development economics* orthodoxy was to grow Gross Domestic Product (GDP)* and to reduce the deficit (the disparity between the value of imports and the value of exports, or between a nation's income and what it spends to support its institutions and infrastructure and so on). Haq argues that this approach to development had not

> ❝ After [World War II]* … an obsession grew with economic growth models and national income accounts. What was important was what could be measured and priced. People as the agents of change and beneficiaries of development were often forgotten. Learned treatises appeared on how to increase production, but little was written on how to enhance human lives. The delinking of ends and means began, with economic science often obsessed with means. ❞
>
> Mahbub ul Haq, *Reflections on Human Development*

improved the situation of people in developing countries. Rather, it had made their lives demonstrably worse.

Haq uses Sri Lanka as an example, writing: "In 1979 an adjustment* package formulated by the [International Monetary Fund*] directed that the free rice rations given to every family be targeted more narrowly … on the very poor through a scheme of food stamps." The scheme backfired, creating corruption and social instability. It resulted in "Sri Lanka … spending more on its policy and its security apparatus than it had spent on food subsidies."[3] The adjustment package—a loan tied to economic reform—was not, in other words, a success; due to this failure of the market-oriented economic philosophy of neoliberalism,* Haq argues that the late 1980s "were ripe for a counteroffensive" against orthodox thinking.[4]

The Participants

In 1990 the British economist John Williamson* published the paper "What Washington Means by Policy Reform." In it, he argues that Washington's approach to development was defined by 10 policy instruments, among which were market liberalization (a decrease in government regulations), increased spending in health and education, and deficit reduction. By "Washington," Williamson means both the American government and the international financial institutions based in Washington: the IMF and the World Bank.*

Williamson calls the policy conditions attached to the aid packages that are given to developing countries[5] the "Washington Consensus";* meaning in effect that aid will only be disbursed if states commit to reform their economies. The policy instruments that Williamson identifies all help to service "the standard economic objectives of growth, low inflation, a visible balance of payments, and an equitable income distribution."[6] This notion of a Washington consensus dominated development thinking when Haq was writing. It's an approach that can be summarized as: the market, free of interference by government, is the basis of a strong and strengthening economy.

The British development economist Richard Jolly* writes: "The World Bank's 1990 *World Development Report* defined the neoliberal approach [to poverty reduction]* as emphasizing economic growth, investment in education and health, and social safety nets." Although the focus was to create a competitive national economy, this approach had little regard to the poor themselves.[7]

There was an alternative model, expounded by the Austrian American academic Paul Streeten:* the basic needs approach* to development, a system concerned with the needs of the poor. It explores needs in economic terms, looking at the commodities people need to survive. "It is true," Streeten writes, "[that] the only way absolute poverty can be eliminated ... is to increase the productivity of the poor. But direct methods to increase the productivity of the poor need to be supplemented with efforts to provide for their unmet basic needs [such as food, shelter, and health]."[8]

The Contemporary Debate
While Haq rejects both the neoliberal approach to development and the basic needs approach, his main concern was to refute the neoliberal

position, the dominant model for development policy at the time when he was writing. In its place, Haq aims to create policies based on human development.*

To do this, Haq needed to change the core question asked by those working in the field of development. In the neoliberal model, the question asked was "How much is the nation producing?" The question Haq wanted to ask was "How are the people of the nation faring?"[9] Once this shift occurred, a more practical question could be asked: how can "growth and distribution policies [be incorporated] in the national planning framework?"[10] This ran counter to the neoliberal orthodoxy, which looked only at policy surrounding growth. In fact, neoliberalism suggested that focusing on distribution, and the government intervention that would go along with it, would only serve to limit growth.

Haq's objection to the basic needs approach was that it focused too much on keeping people alive rather than enabling people to flourish. The basic needs approach eventually became folded into the economic theory known as the capabilities approach,* according to which the goal of politics and economics should be to increase people's capability to live the lives they desire to lead. For Streeten, "the concept of basic needs, as we understood it, was not … centered on the possession of commodities. Instead it was concerned with providing all human beings … with the opportunities for a full life."[11]

NOTES

1   Debraj Ray, *Development Economics* (Princeton: Princeton University Press, 1998), 7.

2   Mahbub ul Haq, *Reflections on Human Development* (Oxford: Oxford University Press, 1995), 24.

3   Mahbub ul Haq, *Reflections on Human Development* (New Delhi: Oxford University Press India, 1999), 145.

4   Haq, *Reflections*, 24.

5   John Williamson, *Latin American Adjustment: How Much Has Happened?*, Peterson Institute of International Economics, 1990, Chapter 2, accessed October 22, 2015, http://www.iie.com/publications/papers/paper. cfm?researchid=486.

6   Williamson, *Latin American Adjustment*.

7   Richard Jolly, "Human Development and Neoliberalism: Paradigms Compared," in *Readings in Human Development*, eds. Sakiko Fukuda-Parr and A. K. Shiva Kumar (New Delhi: Oxford University Press India, 2003), 111.

8   Paul Streeten et al., *First Things First: Meeting Basic Human Needs in Developing Countries* (Washington: World Bank, 1981), VIII.

9   Haq, *Reflections*, 25.

10   Haq, *Reflections*, 8.

11   Streeten, *First Things First*, IX.

MODULE 4
THE AUTHOR'S CONTRIBUTION

KEY POINTS

- Haq argues that development should focus on increasing people's choices rather than solely on economic growth.

- The Human Development Index* (HDI), a numerical index designating life expectancy, education, and wealth, was presented as an alternative indicator of development to Gross Domestic Product* (GDP) growth—a purely economic indicator.

- The HDI was based on the theories of the Indian economist Amartya Sen* and the American philosopher Martha Nussbaum* who argue that societies should be arranged for "human flourishing."*

Author's Aims

Mahbub ul Haq's *Reflections on Human Development* summarizes his work at the helm of the United Nations Development Program (UNDP)'s* *Human Development Report,* the first of which was published in 1990. The first edition of *Reflections on Human Development* was published in 1995, with a second edition following in 1999. As Haq writes, the book "traces my intellectual journey—and the world's—through a profound transition in development thinking in recent years."[1] In effect, his book is about the history of an idea rather than an analytical work.

The *Report* itself had two goals:

- To challenge the neoliberal* growth theory of development.
- To broaden the discipline of development to include Haq's (and Amartya Sen's) more equitable approach to development.

> **❝** The index does, however, have the virtue of incorporating human choices other than income, and consequently is a move in the right direction. It also has the potential for refinement as more aspects of human choice and development are quantified. **❞**
>
> United Nations Development Agency, *Human Development Report 1990*

The American investor William Draper III,* head of the UNDP between 1986 and 1993, wrote the preface to the first *Human Development Report*. He explains that its objective was to "to analyze country experiences to distil practical insights. Its purpose is neither to preach nor to recommend any particular model of development," but rather, to contribute "to the definition, measurement, and policy analysis of human development."*[2] This means that the report did not aim to promote any one particular scheme of development; its aim, instead, was to debunk the idea that equity*—in the sense of economic fairness—must be sacrificed for the sake of growth. It also wanted to broaden the scope of development economics* to include issues of social justice.

Approach

Haq's approach to answering this question was to reformulate what was measured in order to determine a country's development. At the time the most popular metric was Gross Domestic Product (GDP) growth: the extent to which the actual money earned by a country could be grown through things such as industrialization* or free-market growth. This "top level" view entirely ignored how the benefits of growth were distributed. Imagine pushing the concept to its logical limit: if a single person owned all the industry in a country, then the rest of the citizens could live in abject poverty, even if GDP could still rise. GDP, in other words, is flawed as an indicator of development.

As an alternative, Haq devised the Human Development Index (HDI). This gave a numerical figure to a combined measurement of GDP per capita* (per head of population), educational attainment (measured initially in literacy rates and later in average years of schooling), and life expectancy (measured in years).[3] The HDI was not the first attempt to provide a more rounded metric to GDP. In 1975 the Physical Quality of Life Index* was developed for the Washington-based Overseas Development Council, and calculates development based on literacy, infant mortality, and life expectancy.

Haq believed his new index improved on previous indices because it "would measure the basic concept of human development to enlarge people's choices … Obviously, not all these choices could be quantified or measured. The basic idea was to measure at least a few more choices behind income and to reflect them in a methodologically sound composite index."[4]

Contribution in Context

Haq's work goes hand-in-hand with the work of Amartya Sen. Sen argues that the purpose of both politics and economics should be to increase human capabilities, so people can decide what they want to do and who they want to be; Haq is concerned with how this philosophy can be put into practice.

The similarities are most striking in Sen's 1989 essay "Development As Capability Expansion." For Sen, human life can be considered "a set of 'doings and beings'," or "functionings," which relate "the valuation of the quality of life to the assessment of the capability to function."[5] In other words, human life is assessed by what the person can "do and be." A person can "do" cycling and "be" a cyclist if they have the physical capability, political freedom, and income to acquire and use a bicycle as they choose. Sen goes on to assert that Gross National Product* (GNP) growth may not capture this:

"A country can be very rich in conventional economic terms … and still be very poor in the achieved quality of human life." For example, "South Africa, with five or six times the GNP per capita of Sri Lanka or China, has a much lower longevity rate."[6]

The philosopher Martha Nussbaum's Aristotelian-inspired ideas also influenced Haq. For Nussbaum, Aristotle* "was not only a defender of an ethical theory based on the virtues, but also the defender of a single objective account of the human good, or human flourishing [living a life one has reason to value]." Aristotle spoke against moral traditions that were incompatible with human flourishing.[7] Nussbaum argued that "the good" could be understood as that which is in accordance with "virtuousness"—the goal of human flourishing. Haq's work adopts Nussbaum's idea of the good-as-human-flourishing.

NOTES

1   Mahbub ul Haq, *Reflections on Human Development* (New Delhi: Oxford University Press India, 1999), xvii.

2   William H. Draper III, "Foreword," in *Human Development Report 1990* (Oxford: Oxford University Press, 1990), iii.

3   United Nations Development Program, "Human Development Index (HDI)," Human Development Reports, accessed October 22, 2015, http://hdr.undp.org/en/statistics/hdi.

4   Haq, *Reflections*, 47.

5   Amartya Sen, "Development as Capability Expansion," in *Readings in Human Development*, eds. Sakiko Fukuda-Parr and A. K. Shiva Kumar (New Delhi: Oxford University Press India, 2003), 4.

6   Sen, "Development as Capability Expansion," 4.

7   Martha Nussbaum, "Non-Relative Virtues: An Aristotelian Approach," *Midwest Studies of Philosophy* 13, no. 1 (1988): 33.

SECTION 2
IDEAS

MODULE 5
MAIN IDEAS

KEY POINTS

- *Reflections on Human Development* argues against the linking of development and pure growth.

- For Haq, development should be measured with the Human Development Index* (HDI): a numerical figure denoting Gross Domestic Product* (GDP) per head of population, literacy rate, and life expectancy.

- *Reflections* does not offer a technical discussion of development, presenting instead the history of the idea of human development.*

Key Themes

Mahbub ul Haq's *Reflections on Human Development* tells the history of, and explains the theory behind, the United Nations* *Human Development Reports.** In doing so, the book reveals its two key themes:

- The identification of "development" with the "enlargement of real human choices."
- The assertion that GDP growth alone will fail to satisfactorily expand those choices.[1]

Haq puts forward his argument as to why human development—measured by things such as life expectancy, education, and wealth—should become the model for measuring development. In doing so, he offers a resolute critique of the orthodox neoliberal* economic conceptual model.

Haq's overarching argument is that "the basic purpose of development is to enlarge people's choices ... People often value

> " First, the new index would measure the basic concept of human development to enlarge people's choices ... Second, the new index would include only a limited number of variables to keep it simple and manageable ... Third, a composite index would be constructed rather than a plethora of separate indices ... Fourth, the [Human Development Index] would cover both social and economic choices. "
>
> Mahbub ul Haq, *Reflections on Human Development*

achievements that do not show up at all ... in income or growth figures: greater access to knowledge, better nutrition and health services, more secure livelihoods, security against crime and physical violence ... The objective of development is to create an enabling environment for people to enjoy long, healthy, and creative lives."[2] In other words, the main theme of the book is that people should not be seen as a means of increasing a country's national income, as understood according to the neoliberal economic model. Instead, economic growth should be treated as one means among many to improve people's lives.

Exploring the Ideas

As a practitioner of human development, Haq was not purely a theorist; his ideas are best understood through his method of measuring development: the Human Development Index (HDI). The HDI was composed of the following three variables (although these have been adjusted since *Reflections* was published):[3]

- GDP per capita* (that is, per head of population)
- Adult literacy rate and mean (average) years of schooling
- Life expectancy at birth.

The minimum and maximum values of each of these variables are the "most extreme values observed over the previous three decades or expected over the next three decades. These fixed goalposts permit meaningful comparisons of countries' performance over 60 years."[4] Setting aside how well (or not) the HDI works as a measure of development, it was very important as a public relations tool. The HDI broadened the focus of development: the narrow objective of growing a state's income expanded into the objective of growing people's lives.

These ideas were derived from the work of the economist Amartya Sen,* who wrote: "In the context of some types of welfare analysis, for example, in dealing with extreme poverty … we may be able to go a long distance in terms of a relatively small number of centrally important functionings." By this, he means that people's lives can be dramatically changed if some very basic requirements are met. As an example, it is important for people working in development policy to measure life expectancy, as this represents "the ability to be well-nourished and well-sheltered." With nourishment and shelter people have the capability to avoid premature mortality and to grow as a human in other ways.[5]

The HDI was designed to examine how well a state was providing these basic capabilities. Were states using their growth in income to "enlarge people's choices?"[6] If a person wanted to be a writer, for example, but was constantly ill due to poor sanitation, they would be unable to write and their creative ambitions would be thwarted.

Language and Expression

Reflections was written for a mass audience, in largely nontechnical language. Its ideas are, therefore, widely accessible. But the book's nontechnical nature led to criticism by the American professor of

37

economics Michael Kevane.* "Is the book worthwhile?" Kevane asks. He argues that it does not live up to its potential as Haq avoids analyzing the political economy* issues that might illuminate the ways in which societies succeed in improving human well-being.[7] Kevane believes that Haq avoids detailed discussion of difficult policy recommendations in favor of a more general story of the human development paradigm (that is, conceptual model).

In the first part of *Reflections*, "Towards a New Development Paradigm," Haq looks at the history of development, beginning by outlining the orthodox development approach and how it needed to be challenged. He outlines the emergence of the human development paradigm, then briefly summarizes the content and focus of each report. He goes on to discuss the methodology behind the reports—the Human Development Index (HDI). He discusses two ways in which the HDI could be expanded: by including measurements that relate to political freedom and environmental sustainability. Haq concludes the first part of the book with a discussion of how these principles could be applied to help South Asia and the Islamic world.

In the second part, "Towards a New International Dialogue," Haq offers a less-organized discussion of various issues that relate to development; one such is human security*—not simply "security" in the sense of safety from the effects of violence between states, but also security from issues such as poverty and ill-health. Another is the "20:20 development compact"*: for developing nations receiving foreign aid, 20 percent of that aid and 20 percent of the nation's existing budget should be earmarked for social concerns.

Haq concludes the book with a discussion of his vision of a supranational* development body (a cross-border development body with influence over the governments of individual states).

NOTES

1   Mahbub ul Haq, *Reflections on Human Development* (Oxford: Oxford University Press, 1995), 14.

2   Haq, *Reflections*, 14.

3   Haq, *Reflections*, 49.

4   Haq, *Reflections*, 50.

5   Amartya Sen, "Development as Capability Expansion," in *Readings in Human Development*, eds. Sakiko Fukuda-Parr and A. K. Shiva Kumar (New Delhi: Oxford University Press India, 2003), 6.

6   Haq, *Reflections*, 14.

7   Michael Kevane, "*Reflections on Human Development* by Mahbub ul Haq," *Journal of Economic Literature* 35, no. 1 (1997): 178.

MODULE 6
SECONDARY IDEAS

KEY POINTS

- Haq's secondary ideas relate to governments and the importance of political freedom for human development.*

- One sub-theme of the book is "human security."* Haq's definition of this term does not relate to "national security" in the sense of state-to-state violence, but to individuals' concerns about issues such as sanitation, poverty, and ill-health.

- Haq says that 20 percent of foreign aid from developed countries should be earmarked for social concerns, as should 20 percent of a developing country's budget. This idea, the "20:20 compact,"* has been overlooked.

Other Ideas

The key secondary themes of Mahbub ul Haq's *Reflections on Human Development* relate to security and freedom. Haq used the term human security to refer to security issues that go beyond interstate aggression. These issues include the spread of disease, regional instability, and access to food—a central concern raised in the 1994 *Human Development Report.** That report called for an expansion of the concept of security and the development of a human security paradigm. *Reflections* addressed these ideas.

Another important, if subordinate, theme in the book centers on Haq's advocacy of political participation across a state—not just within its big cities. He argues that this is a core part of sustainable development,* and requires both freedom and decentralization (that is, moving authority from one central body to other non-central bodies e.g. regional/municipal government). Developing countries

> 66 The developing countries would commit an average of 20 percent of their budgets to human priority concerns rather than the present 10 percent—by reducing military expenditures, by privatizing inefficient public enterprises, and by eliminating low-priority development expenditure. The rich nations would raise their human-priority allocations from the present 7 percent of ODA [Official Development Assistance] to around 20 percent. 99
>
> Mahbub ul Haq, *Reflections on Human Development*

have to become democratic: "People must be empowered to guide both the state and the market—to serve the interests of the people."[1] He also argues that "most developing countries are over-centralized." On average, less than 10 percent of national budgets actually pass beyond the major urban areas because "decision-making is kept in the hands of a small, central elite."[2]

Haq's argument for greater participation in politics is based on his belief that human development is inseparable from basic freedoms, writing: "Life expectancy and literacy could be quite high in a well-managed prison. Basic physical needs are well met in a zoo," and "freedom cannot be separated from human development."[3] He acknowledged this is obvious: if development is to be a question of expanding human choice, political choice is an important part of this. Haq also believed, however, that measuring such a variable was difficult to achieve. Incorporating it in the Human Development Index* would be even more difficult.[4]

Exploring the Ideas

The traditional definition of "security" is bound up in the state-driven military control of territory. Haq's term "human security" describes a need for security from a wide variety of threats: security "of people, not just territory; security of individuals, not just nations; security through development, not through arms; security of all the people everywhere— in their homes, in their jobs, in their streets, in their communities, in their environment."[5] In other words, human security sees state invasion as one security risk among many. It views social instability, disease, and famine as greater risks because they make people's lives worse.

Drawing on this, Haq criticized the balance of military and social spending of many nations. He urged countries in the developed world to close their military bases abroad and halt arms exports to poorer countries. He also called for countries in the developing world to ask important questions such as "Why do we have 20 times more soldiers than doctors?"[6] Human security has become a paradigm in itself, debated in security studies.

Political freedom, Haq acknowledges, is difficult to measure. In 1992, a new index was introduced into the annual *Human Development Report*: the Political Freedom Index* (PFI).

The PFI was based on political participation, rule of law, freedom of expression, and nondiscrimination. The index measured indicators such as the continuity and sustainability of democratic institutions, presumption of innocence until proven guilty, independent ownership and control of media, as well as a lack of discrimination based on gender.[7] This trial index ranked 100 nations—with Sweden as the most free and Iraq as the least free. Haq, however, had reservations. He commented that "work must proceed in many academic institutions to further refine a political freedom index before it can be used with confidence and before it can be merged with the more established [Human Development Index]."[8]

Overlooked

The last section of Haq's text puts forward his plan to "make human development happen."This later became known as the 20:20 compact.

Haq proposed that both 20 percent of foreign aid from developed countries and 20 percent of the budgets of developing countries should be earmarked for social concerns; this, he believed, would provide a framework that prioritized human development. Indeed, Haq had claimed that reallocating (not increasing) Official Development Assistance* (ODA)—the sum of money set aside by a government to transfer to the developing world, either directly or through institutions such as the World Bank* or European Union—in donor countries and internal development budgets in recipient countries would achieve all the literacy, life expectancy, and related goals of the human development paradigm.

The root of Haq's redistributive plan is found in the *Human Development Report 1991.* In this Haq wrote: "The arithmetic is simple. Official development assistance for all countries currently represents 0.32 percent of their combined GNP.* Of this, only 23 percent went to social sectors in 1988, and of the social sector spending, only 37 percent went to human development priority areas."[9] In 1994 Haq argued that achieving all of human development's social goals "would require additional spending on the order of $30 to $40 billion a year." The money could be found by reprioritizing existing aid budgets using the 20:20 compact: "Required is a 20:20 compact on human development—under which 20 percent of developing country budgets and 20 percent of industrial country aid are allocated to human priority expenditure."[10]

Considering the numbers given in 1991, this is a significant proposed shift indeed. But this idea has largely been overlooked. According to the American professor of economics Michael Kevane,* the 20:20 compact "should have been the central concept of the book, bolstered by an analysis quantifying the improvements in the HDI, especially in terms of the trade-off between possibly slower [Gross National Product] growth and faster progress in literacy and life expectancy. Instead we find it buried in chapter 15, almost an afterthought."[11]

NOTES

1   Mahbub ul Haq, *Reflections on Human Development* (New Delhi: Oxford University Press India, 1999), 36.

2   Haq, *Reflections*, 37.

3   Haq, *Reflections*, 67.

4   Haq, *Reflections* 67–8.

5   Haq, *Reflections*, 115.

6   Haq, *Reflections*, 118.

7   Mahbub ul Haq, *Reflections on Human Development* (Oxford: Oxford University Press, 1995), 70.

8   Haq, *Reflections*, 72.

9   UNDP, *Human Development Report 1991* (New York: Oxford University Press, 1991), 56.

10 UNDP, *Human Development Report 1994* (New York: Oxford University Press, 1994), 77.

11 Michael Kevane, "*Reflections on Human Development* by Mahbub ul Haq," *Journal of Economic Literature* 35, no. 1 (1997): 177.

MODULE 7
ACHIEVEMENT

KEY POINTS

- Haq's work turned "human development"* into the new orthodoxy in the field of development.

- The World Bank* and International Monetary Fund* (IMF) accepted that economic growth does not automatically "trickle down"* after experiencing their own development issues.

- The human development paradigm has been criticized for making "Western liberal" assumptions about what people see as important.

Assessing the Argument

Mahbub ul Haq's *Reflections on Human Development*, and the *Human Development Reports** that the book is based on, have changed the way development is practiced. Haq's work has influenced institutions and countries to change their approach to development. The most visible sign of that was the adoption of the Millennium Development Goals* by the United Nations.* These were eight international development goals which included universal primary education and the eradication of poverty and hunger.

The impact of Haq's work is also clear on a country level: over 700 *Human Development Reports* have been prepared since 1992 at national, regional, and local levels from 135 countries.[1] Vietnam, for example, has authored several *Human Development Reports* to guide its own internal development policy. "[Ten] years ago," the 2011 *Report* begins, "the very first Vietnam *Human Development Report* was launched. It focused on the *doi moi** policy reforms [which saw the transition from

> ❝ The real impact of the report can be seen in the human development strategies that many developing countries have begun to formulate. Several countries have taken major steps on the road to formulating and implementing their own long-term human development plans. ❞
>
> Mahbub ul Haq, *Reflections on Human Development*

a socialist to a free-market economy] and their impact on poverty reduction* and human development," but "a new development approach is … needed if Vietnam wants to achieve better quality, sustainable growth."[2]

Vietnam had been an early adopter of this model, enshrining in its constitution "the people's rights as masters in all spheres" and "the targets of building a prosperous life for its people."[3] The report notes: "The Government of Vietnam uses changes in the [Human Development Index]* and [Gender-related Development Index]* over time as an indicator of progress towards human development and gender equality."[4]

Achievement in Context
As the concept of human development became broader, two related developments occurred:
- The range of political and social issues addressed by development coalesced into a rhetorical consensus on "poverty reduction."
- Human development became mainstream.

"Poverty reduction" was formally enshrined in the Organization of Economic Cooperation and Development* (OECD)'s policy document of 1996, "Shaping the 21st Century: The Contribution of Development Cooperation."[5] This defined its economic objective not as financial growth but as "a reduction by one-half in the proportion of people living in extreme poverty by 2015."[6] In consequence, as the development economist Sakiko Fukuda-Parr* notes: "Development discourses today can no longer be so clearly characterized as to be divided between the 'growth school' and the 'people-centered' school as Mahbub ul Haq had done in 1990." The idea that development should be harnessed to meet the needs of the people, broadly conceived as reducing poverty, was now mainstream thinking.[7]

The ambition of the OECD was further elevated in 2000 with the eight Millennium Development Goals:

- To eradicate poverty and hunger
- To achieve universal primary education
- To promote gender equality
- To reduce child mortality
- To improve maternal health
- To combat disease
- To ensure environmental sustainability
- To develop a global partnership for development.

Fukuda-Parr notes that these goals "are used by all major stakeholders in the international development community ... as the overarching global goals for international development."[8]

Limitations

The most contentious aspect of Haq's work is whether the principles that guided him were truly "universal" and "timeless." The concept of human development is strongly influenced by the political philosophy of liberalism,* with its emphasis on individual liberty and free choice, particularly Western-style liberal democracy.

This is criticized by the Dutch academic Jan Nederveen Pieterse.*
His criticism centers on the 2004 *Human Development Report*, which
argued that "defending tradition can hold back human development."
The report also said that some cultural institutions should not exist if
they deny people the capability "to live as they would choose, with
adequate opportunity to consider other options."[9] Pieterse says this
is problematic: "In approach and language it reads like an American
take on culture and development."[10] There is a paradox, he points
out, at the center of the report—and indeed in the human
development approach to non-liberal cultures; the report "wants all-
around cultural inclusion—but not cultural conservatism; it wants a
multicultural democracy—but not cultural conservatism ... In effect
this takes the politics out of culture and identity."[11]

Pieterse is not the only critic of human development along these
lines. The Indian thinker and novelist Ratan Lal Basu* criticizes the
field's preoccupation with material well-being; material provisions,
he writes, "are inseparable from human development efforts, but
they themselves are not human development, which, according to
ancient Indian literature, is the process of ethical and spiritual
development of human beings."[12] According to Basu's interpretation
of the traditional Indian position, the Human Development Index is
good for preserving humans as animals, but not for actually
developing them as spiritual creatures. For Basu, "the theories
developed by [Amartya Sen],* Haq, and others on the basis of a
Western commercial world outlook, end up in the provision of
material conditions for decent animal-living."[13] Basu believes that
the true definition of "human development" is bound up by being
"satva"*—displaying "abstinence, self-sacrifice, love, philanthropy,
mercy, self-confidence, diligence, and composure" in a high degree.[14]

There is much more than material provision, or simple freedom
of choice, in this interpretation of development.

NOTES

1   UNDP, "About the Reports," Human Development Reports, accessed October 21, 2015, http://hdr.undp.org/en/content/about-reports.

2   UNDP, *Social Services for Human Development: Vietnam Human Development Report 2011* (Hanoi: United Nations, 2011), iv.

3   UNDP, *Vietnam Human Development Report 2011*, 11.

4   UNDP, *Vietnam Human Development Report 2011*, 12.

5   Mahbub ul Haq, *Reflections on Human Development* (New Delhi: Oxford University Press India, 1999), 25.

6   Organization of Economic Cooperation and Development, *Shaping the 21st Century: The Contribution of Development Cooperation* (Paris: OECD, 1996), 2.

7   Sakiko Fukuda-Parr, "The Intellectual Journey Continues," in *Pioneering the Human Development Revolution: An Intellectual Biography of Mahbub ul Haq*, eds. Khadija Haq and Richard Ponzio (Oxford: Oxford University Press, 2008), 248.

8   Sakiko Fukuda-Parr, "Theory and Policy in International Development: Human Development and Capability Approach and the Millennium Development Goals," *International Studies Review* 13, no. 1 (2011): 123.

9   UNDP, *Human Development Report 2004: Cultural Liberty in Today's Diverse World* (New York: Oxford University Press, 2004), 17.

10 Jan Nederveen Pieterse, "The *Human Development Report* and Cultural Liberty: Tough Liberalism," *Development and Change* 36, no. 6 (2005): 1272.

11 Nederveen Pieterse, "The *Human Development Report* and Cultural Liberty," 1271.

12 Ratan Lal Basu, "Why the Human Development Index Does Not Live up to Ancient Indian Standards," *Culture Mandala* 6, no. 2 (2005): 3.

13 Basu, "Ancient Indian Standards," 5.

14 Basu, "Ancient Indian Standards," 3.

MODULE 8
PLACE IN THE AUTHOR'S WORK

KEY POINTS

- Haq's work has always focused on economic development.

- Haq's early writings were more in line with the "growth focus" approach to development, which he later rejected in favor of his "people-centered" approach.

- Haq's work has been enormously influential. It opened human development* as a field of study, and promoted real change among policy makers.

Positioning

There are two editions of Mahbub ul Haq's *Reflections on Human Development*. The first was published in 1995 and the second, posthumously, in 1999. Haq died in July 1998, so both editions of his seminal work came at the end of an enormously influential career. Haq was a prolific writer of books and journal articles, and published several important policy papers. But while *Reflections* is a summary of his work, his greatest contribution to development were the *Human Development Reports*,* written for the United Nations.* Haq oversaw these for six years, from their inception in 1990 until 1996. These reports are the main focus of *Reflections*.

Haq's other writing discussed how to reform and strengthen global governance* through existing institutions—namely the International Monetary Fund* (IMF) and the World Bank.* These monetary management institutions were founded in 1944 at an international conference at the Bretton Woods resort in the United States. They are known as the Bretton Woods Institutions.*

In the co-edited volume *The UN and the Bretton Woods Institutions* (1995), Haq and his colleagues discuss the conclusions of the North-

> ❝ Over the thirteen years of my association with Pakistan's economic planning, I was forced to reconsider many of [my] views as my convictions clashed with facts ... Pakistan's decade of rapid economic development during the 1960s was beginning to crumble, not because of the pace of growth in the Gross National Product had been insufficient, but *in spite of* an enviable record of growth. ❞
>
> Mahbub ul Haq, *The Poverty Curtain*

South Roundtable,* a forum for development policy cooperation between donor and recipient states to facilitate the future of development. This group called for "a world social charter" that would bind the globe's countries in a compact of mutual solidarity—akin to social support that exists within states in the form of, say, welfare payments, or credits for food or medical treatment. The Roundtable also suggested "a development security council." This would administer economic development in a manner akin to the UN Security Council*—the highest authority in the United Nations.[1] The idea was that the council would set the overarching strategy, with much of the work carried out through existing Bretton Woods Institutions by expanding their lending capacities and shifting their priorities.

Integration

Early in his career, Haq's thought shifted from orthodox, largely neoliberal* growth theories of development to more socially conscious theories based on human development. His first book, *The Strategy of Economic Planning* (1963), took a traditionalist view toward growth and development: "It is well to recognize that economic growth is a brutal, sordid process ... The essence of it lies in making the laborer produce more than he is allowed to consume for his immediate needs, and to invest and reinvest the surplus thus obtained."[2]

What changed Haq's mind was seeing what happened when Pakistan went through an impressive period of growth. Instead of benefitting the country as a whole, this growth concentrated much of the national income surplus in the hands of just 22 families. Seeing this prompted Haq to shift from a growth approach to development to a poverty reduction* approach.[3] By the time he published *The Poverty Curtain* in 1976, Haq had concluded that "the most unforgivable sin of development planners is to become mesmerized by high growth rates in the gross national produce and to forget the real objective of development."[4]

With this in mind, Haq led the production of the first *Human Development Report* in 1990. "The central message of this *Human Development Report* is that while [growth in Gross Domestic Product]* is absolutely necessary to meet all essential human objectives, what is important is to study how this growth translates—or fails to translate— into human development in various societies."[5]

Significance

"Amartya Sen* has rightly designated Mahbub ul Haq as 'the pioneering leader of the human development approach,'" wrote the German development economist Gustav Ranis* and British academic Frances Stewart.*[6] Since the production of the first *Human Development Report* in 1990, Haq's influence has been enormous. As the British development economist Richard Jolly* observed: "Within a year or two, many individual countries began producing their own human development reports, applying the paradigm to their own national platforms and policies"; the human development approach became a major contender as the dominant model in international development, defining the development policy of the United Nations.[7] It was not Haq's book, *Reflections*, that engendered this shift but the *Human Development Report* itself.

The effect of Haq's work on development has affected the living standards of citizens in developing countries worldwide. His ideas have created nothing less than an intellectual revolution. "The intellectual journey that Mahbub started several decades ago," writes Sakiko Fukuda-Parr,* "continues in development policy as well as academic research." Haq's work has led to the formation of academic-practice alliances, including the Human Development and Capability Association.* This is a community of academics and practitioners who seek to keep human development at the forefront of policy and planning. And in the Pakistani capital of Islamabad, Haq set up a think tank called the Mahbub ul Haq Human Development Center* to promote human development in South Asia.[8]

NOTES

1   Mahbub ul Haq et al., *The UN and the Bretton Woods Institutions: New Challenges for the Twenty-First Century* (New York: Macmillan, 1995), 9–12.

2   Mahbub ul Haq, *The Strategy of Economic Planning* (Oxford: Oxford University Press, 1963), 1.

3   Mahbub ul Haq, *The Poverty Curtain: Choices for the Third World* (New York: Columbia University Press, 1976), 7.

4   Haq, *The Poverty Curtain*, 25.

5   William H. Draper III, "Foreword," in *Human Development Report 1990* (Oxford: Oxford University Press, 1990), iii.

6   Gustav Ranis and Frances Stewart, "Successful Transition Towards a Virtuous Cycle of Human Development and Economic Growth: Country Studies," Economic Growth Center, Yale University (2006), accessed October 21, 2015, http://www.econ.yale.edu/growth_pdf/cdp943.pdf.

7   Richard Jolly et al., *UN Ideas that Changed the World* (Indianapolis: Indiana University Press, 2009), 187.

8   Sakiko Fukuda-Parr, "The Intellectual Journey Continues," in *Pioneering the Human Development Revolution: An Intellectual Biography of Mahbub ul Haq*, eds. Khadija Haq and Richard Ponzio (Oxford: Oxford University Press, 2008), 252.

SECTION 3
IMPACT

MODULE 9
THE FIRST RESPONSES

KEY POINTS

- The Human Development Index* (HDI) was criticized for being methodologically problematic.

- The HDI was altered in response to criticism. It was made more methodologically rigorous by altering what was being measured (years of schooling rather than literacy rate, for example).

- The HDI was also criticized for being ideological—reflecting political and social assumptions, for example—rather than functional. It was later clarified that the HDI was as important for drawing attention to human development* as it was for rigorously measuring development.

Criticism

The key contribution made by Mahbub ul Haq, author of *Reflections on Human Development*, was to create the Human Development Index. This composite index shows a country's overall state of "human development" by measuring the life expectancy, education, and wealth of its citizens.

The initial criticism made about the HDI focused primarily on its methodology; the Indian academic A. D. Sagar* and the Pakistani academic A. Najam* write, for example: "We share the [*Human Development Reports*] general philosophy of expanding the scope of the development discussion beyond just measures of income. However we have a number of concerns about its translation into an index."[1] This concern was voiced more widely. The methodological criticism has been largely constructive; Sagar and Najam's position

> ❝ First, it would be a great mistake to concentrate too much on the Human Development Index, or on any other such aggregative index ... These are useful indicators in rough and ready work, but the real merit of the human development approach lies in the plural attention it brings to bear on developmental evaluation, not in the aggregative measures it presents as an aid to digestion of diverse statistics. ❞
>
> Amartya Sen, "A Decade of Human Development"

that the HDI has a noble purpose but needs improvement is representative of most critiques.

A more fundamental criticism comes from the Australian academic Mark McGillivray.* He argues that the HDI "generally reveals little more than any one of the preexisting development indicators alone reveals."[2] The three variables it measures (life expectancy, education, and wealth) are often present at similar rates in similar places. This means measuring just one of these variables would produce similar rankings to those found in the composite index.[3] Rather than being the best way to measure development, McGillivray believes the HDI is a largely ideological device that advances the cause of social development rather than offering "new insights into intercountry development levels."[4]

The Indian economist T. N. Srinivasan* argues that the HDI "is conceptually weak and empirically unsound, involving serious problems of noncomparability over time and space, measurement errors, and biases."[5] One key criticism highlights the fundamental noncomparability of the HDI; according to Srinivasan, "relative values need not be the same across individuals, countries, and socioeconomic groups."[6]

Responses

Haq responded positively to the first set of methodological critiques. He modified the HDI between the first report in 1990 and the second in the following year.[7] Then, in the 1994 report, the HDI was modified further. "Goalposts were fixed for each indicator," at 30 years before and after measurement, "to allow comparison over time."[8]

Other critics questioned not only how human development was measured, but whether or not it was even worth measuring. These criticisms prompted rebuttal rather than accommodation. But Haq was not an academic; he was a policy maker, and so his response to these criticisms was indirect.

The epilogue to the 1999 edition of *Reflections* sheds some light on what he believed to be the real use of the HDI. Here, he discusses "changing the overall environment in which policies are formulated." This seems to suggest that the HDI was designed primarily to show that there was more to development than income growth.[9] The influential economist Amartya Sen* clarified that the HDI was used "mainly as an instrument of public communication ...We have to see the human development index as a deliberately constructed crude measure, offered as a rival to the GNP* ... But it is extremely important not to read more into the HDI than is there."[10] In other words, criticism of the HDI on methodological grounds is valid. The methodology for changing the HDI has changed over time to reflect this. The true significance of the HDI, however, was the way in which it fundamentally reoriented the development debate.

Conflict and Consensus

There was widespread criticism of the HDI on the grounds that it was not statistically rigorous. Despite that, the consensus on the *Human Development Reports* generally and the HDI specifically, was that they represented a "step forward" in development measurement. It broadened the range of what it was legitimate to measure.[11]

The HDI has continued to be refined. The Australian economist Martin Ravallion* writes: "From 1990 to 2000 the HDI gave equal (linear) weights to three functions of its core dimensions for health, education, and income." The indicators and weighting changed in 2010.[12] Where the pre-2010 HDI measured the logarithm* of Gross Domestic Product* (GDP) per capita,* the post-2010 HDI measured Gross National Income* per capita.[13] For the education component, "literacy and the gross enrollment rate have been replaced by mean years of schooling and expected years of schooling."[14]

However, the most significant change in the way the HDI is now calculated is in the weighting (adjustments made). The old method of calculation that took the arithmetic mean* (the average of a set of numbers, calculated by adding each number and dividing by the total number of figures) of the rating between 0 and 1 of each indicator was replaced by the geometric mean* (calculated by multiplying the numbers of the set together; the nth root—where n is the number of numbers—is then taken of the product). This allowed results to be interpreted more clearly. The fact that the reports continue to be published and the HDI continues to be adjusted suggests that Haq's work (as summarized in *Reflections*) is still relevant today.

NOTES

1   A. D. Sagar and A. Najam, "The Human Development Index: A Critical Review," *Ecological Economics* 25, no. 3 (1998): 251.

2   Mark McGillivray, "The Human Development Index: Yet Another Redundant Composite Indicator?" *World Development* 19, no. 10 (1991): 1461.

3   McGillivray, "The Human Development Index," 1467.

4   McGillivray, "The Human Development Index," 1467.

5   T. N. Srinivasan, "Human Development: A New Paradigm or Reinvention of the Wheel?" *The American Economic Review* 84, no. 2 (1994): 241.

6   Srinivasan, "Human Development," 240.

7   Sagar and Najam, "The Human Development Index," 251.

8   Sagar and Najam, "The Human Development Index," 251.

9   Mahbub ul Haq, *Reflections on Human Development* (New Delhi: Oxford University Press India, 1999), 223.

10 Amartya Sen, "Foreword," in *Readings in Human Development*, eds. Sakiko Fukuda-Parr and A. K. Shiva Kumar (New Delhi: Oxford University Press India, 2003), x.

11 Amartya Sen, "A Decade of Human Development," *Journal of Human Development* 1, no. 1 (2000): 21.

12 Martin Ravallion, "Troubling Trade-offs in the Human Development Index," *Journal of Development Economics* 99, no. 2 (2012): 201.

13 Ravallion, "Troubling Trade-offs," 202.

14 Ravallion, "Troubling Trade-offs," 202.

MODULE 10
THE EVOLVING DEBATE

KEY POINTS

- Since *Reflections* was written, new indicators of human development* have been introduced. These measure gender issues, poverty, and freedom.

- The capability approach* to development—a political philosophy according to which politics and economics should be increasing our capacity to decide rationally what we want to be and to do—is now a coherent school of thought. It centers on *Development as Freedom* (1999) by Amartya Sen.*

- Haq's goal of making development more beneficial to "the people" led to greater concern with the relationship between gender and economics.

Uses and Problems

In *Reflections on Human Development*, Mahbub ul Haq discusses the Human Development Index* (HDI) as a tool for measuring human development.

Since it was first introduced in the United Nation's *Human Development Report* of 1990, the HDI has been subject to ongoing refinement. New indices have been used to capture and promote new ideas. The *Human Development Reports* from 1995 and 1997 focused on measuring gender equality and poverty, respectively creating the Gender-related Development Index* (GDI) and Human Poverty Index* (HPI). The GDI adjusted a country's HDI for gender disparity (inequalities between men and women),[1] while the HPI, measuring deprivation, used the same three categories employed by the HDI to measure development.[2]

> **"** Expansion of freedom is viewed, in this approach, both as the primary end and as the principal means of development. Development consists of the removal of various types of unfreedoms that leave people with little choice and little opportunity of exercising their reasoned agency. **"**
>
> Amartya Sen, *Development as Freedom*

Since 2000, the reports have become less concerned with economic and social issues. Instead, their scope has broadened to encompass a policy agenda around human rights and democracy. The development economist Sakiko Fukuda-Parr* notes that composite indices were not created in these areas because the team was "wary of the perverse power of the HDI in reducing the complex concept of human development to a simple index."[3]

Fukuda-Parr also writes that "these reports expanded the scope of the HD agenda by adding two pillars—political participation and multiculturalism."[4] The reports invite a broad discussion of human rights, with the *Human Development Report* of 2000 beginning: "Human rights and human development share a common vision and a common purpose—to secure the freedom, well-being, and dignity of all people everywhere."[5]

Schools of Thought

While the human development paradigm is often identified with Haq, it is also influenced by the work of Amartya Sen* and Martha Nussbaum.* Haq's work is based on Sen's capability approach. This political philosophy emphasizes that the aim of politics and economics should be to increase humans' capabilities: our opportunity to decide what we want to be.

Sen remains a major figure within the human development school of thought, as does Nussbaum, who is often credited as its co-founder. Sen's book *Development as Freedom* (1999) is seminal to the discipline. It argues that "development can be seen as a process of expanding the real freedoms that people enjoy."[6] "Development can be seen," writes Sen, "as a process of expanding human freedom." This is in direct contrast to "standard" approaches that "[identify] development with the growth of Gross National Product."[*7]

Sen's approach emphasizes that people suffer limited freedom because their capabilities are limited by their circumstances. These circumstances include low income, but they are not limited to economic factors alone. "A person who is denied the opportunity of employment but given a handout from the state as an 'unemployment benefit'" may have his or her basic needs provided for, and therefore "look a lot less deprived in the space of incomes than in terms of the valuable ... opportunity of having a fulfilling occupation."[8] However, this person may have a poverty of opportunities. For example: perhaps they cannot read, and do not have the opportunity to learn. This person is poor in a nonmaterial sense. Sen's capability approach sees both poverty and development as multidimensional. Growth is important, but it is only a means to an end. That end is the goal of expanding freedom by developing human capabilities by, say, building schools.

In Current Scholarship

Fukuda-Parr is a prolific commentator on Haq and human development generally. She has also written extensively on a feminist interpretation of the capability approach. A key concern of feminist development is the "feminization of poverty." This is the idea that women are more vulnerable to poverty (and make up a disproportionately large segment of the world's poor). In 2005 the American academic Martha Chen* wrote a report for the United

Nations Development Fund for Women* (UNIFEM). This report, *Progress of the World's Women 2005*, highlighted three ways in which poverty is gendered. According to Chen, "the proportion of women workers engaged in informal employment* is generally greater than the proportion of men workers; women are concentrated in the more precarious types of informal employment; and the average earnings from these types of informal employment are too low, in the absence of other sources of income, to raise households out of poverty."[9]

Fukuda-Parr says that using a capability-based human development approach to gender equity shows that women are not just at an economic disadvantage. The problems go deeper: "Women's 'poverty' in the human development approach goes beyond the lack of income to deprivation in capabilities, such as lack of education, health, and the channels to participate in economic life and in decision-making."[10]

Fukuda-Parr highlights that more human-centered measurement can capture the "feminization of poverty" in ways that household consumption and income surveys cannot: "When asked to identify individuals in the community who are 'poor,' people consistently pointed to women. Even women who commanded considerable wealth and income were included [because] they do not enjoy autonomy in decision-making."[11]

NOTES

1   UNDP, *Human Development Report 1995* (New York: Oxford University Press, 1995), 73.

2   UNDP, *Human Development Report 1997* (New York: Oxford University Press, 1997),18.

3   Sakiko Fukuda-Parr, "The Intellectual Journey Continues," in *Pioneering the Human Development Revolution: An Intellectual Biography of Mahbub ul Haq*, eds. Khadija Haq and Richard Ponzio (Oxford: Oxford University Press, 2008), 232.

4   Fukuda-Parr, "The Intellectual Journey Continues," 243.

5   UNDP, *Human Development Report 2000* (New York: Oxford University Press, 2000),18.

6   Amartya Sen, *Development as Freedom* (Oxford: Oxford University Press, 1999), 3.

7   Sen, *Development as Freedom*, 1.

8   Sen, *Development as Freedom*, 94.

9   Martha Chen et al., *Progress of the World's Women 2005* (New York: United Nations Development Fund for Women, 2005), 8.

10 Sakiko Fukuda-Parr, "The Human Development Paradigm: Operationalizing Sen's Ideas on Capabilities," *Feminist Economics* 9, nos. 2–3 (2003): 314.

11 Sakiko Fukuda-Parr, "What Does Feminization of Poverty Mean? It isn't Just Lack of Income," *Feminist Economics* 5, no. 2 (1999): 102.

MODULE 11
IMPACT AND INFLUENCE TODAY

KEY POINTS

- Haq's work inspired the United Nations Millennium Development Goals* in 2000.

- Haq's ideas are challenged by other thinkers such as the South Korean institutional economist Ha-Joon Chang.* Chang argues that the first priority of development is to build industry, rather than "good lives."

- Ha-Joon Chang argues that the human development* approach makes the life of the poor more bearable, but it does not open up real opportunities.

Position

Mahbub ul Haq's book *Reflections on Human Development* prompted significant advances in the field of international development. Today those advances can be seen in the development targets proposed by the United Nations:* the Millennium Development Goals (MDGs) and the new Sustainable Development Goals* (SDGs), which focus on mitigating the impact of development on the environment. The MDGs specified eight goals, from the eradication of hunger to the development of a "global partnership for development." All UN member states and 23 international organizations were urged to achieve these goals by 2015.[1]

Some human development theorists have, however, become suspicious of the MDGs. The American economist William Easterly,* for example, believes that the MDGs display a strong anti-Africa bias. For him, "the MDGs are poorly and arbitrarily designed to measure progress against poverty and deprivation, and their design makes Africa

> " Goal 1: Eradicate Hunger and Extreme Poverty
> Goal 2: Achieve Universal Primary Education
> Goal 3: Promote Gender Equality and Empower Women
> Goal 4: Reduce Child Mortality
> Goal 5: Improve Maternal Health
> Goal 6: Combat HIV/AIDS, Malaria, and Other Diseases
> Goal 7: Ensure Environmental Sustainability
> Goal 8: Develop a Global Partnership for Development. "
>
> United Nations, *Millennium Development Goals*

look worse than it really is."[2] His criticism is that the MDGs create a broad range of ways in which African countries can be portrayed as struggling. As a result, the MDGs become an ideological tool that keeps Africa dependent on the West.

The development academic Charles Gore* takes a more sympathetic view of the MDGs. He believes that the MDGs are "immensely significant" because of "the emergence of a global consciousness in which persons all over the world are seen as living in a single social space and the nature of their well-being is compared." This development view links social ills such as poverty, insecurity, terrorism, and health into a single web of issues.[3] But Gore believes that the MDGs remain problematic; for him, "the new international development consensus has been achieved through the elimination of the old idea of promoting national economic development."[4]

Although the MDGs are popular, then, it is clear that they are not universally accepted.

Interaction

As well as responding to MDG skeptics like Gore, those who follow the capability* paradigm associated with the thinkers Amartya Sen* and Martha Nussbaum* also have to address the challenge of "growth"-oriented approaches. The South Korean institutional economist Ha-Joon Chang believes in the East Asian model* of development. According to this approach, human development has to be preceded by an increase in productive capacity; the goal of poverty reduction* will then follow.[5] In effect, Chang is willing to accept low human development outcomes or political authoritarianism—governmental interference in the lives of individuals—in order to create industrialization* (a move to an economy based on industrial production) and productivity.

Sakiko Fukuda-Parr* argues that theories like Chang's miss the point. For her, "the MDGs are not a technocratically defined set of goals" but "a global commitment and a framework for accountability"[6] ("technocratic" refers to a system of governance based on theoretical or technical competence, particularly in industrial and economic matters). In other words, the MDGs are intended to set the thinking of the international development community and to put people at the center of development projects.

Fukuda-Parr and the British academic David Hulme* explained the power of the MDGs to shape pro-poor policy in a more general way. They used the model of international norm dynamics* developed by the American international relations academics Martha Finnemore* and Kathryn Sikkink.* This model holds that norms (simply, things considered normal) are thought of and declared by international actors (that is, people operating at an international level). If enough actors adopt the norm, then it has "cascaded" and becomes a legitimate goal. Eventually, conformity with the norm becomes so natural that the norm no longer needs to be actively promoted. So the broad acceptance of the MDGs represents a global consensus that "dehumanizing poverty is morally unacceptable and should be eradicated."[7]

While Fukuda-Parr welcomes the "normative shift" that has followed from the MDGs, she believes that "it is far from evident that the implementation strategies have undergone the same shift."[8] The language of the MDGs has been implemented at a donor and country level, but "what is striking is the absence of the strategic elements of the [human development approach]," namely, employment, natural resource conservation, and political representation.

The Continuing Debate

Chang is a statist thinker: he believes that the state should control either economic or social policy, or both. Statist thinkers criticize the human development approach for assuming an automatic link between social development (education, health care, and human rights) and "actual" development, defined by Chang as "the acquisition of more productive knowledge."[9]

For Chang, projects like the MDGs have development the wrong way round. Good institutions, such as democracy, rule of law, and human rights do not engender development. Instead, economic development (a growth in productivity) leads to good institutions.[10] "Laudable though [the MDGs] may be … they pay no serious attention to the transformation of productive structures and capabilities," he writes.[11] His argument is that although the MDGs focus on making life bearable for citizens of the least developed countries, they do not build the capacity of these citizens to grow their own economies. They will be healthy, well-educated, and well-governed, but it is just assumed that real productivity will follow automatically from these conditions.

Chang pointed out that "growth in the East Asian economies is also notable in that it has resulted in remarkable improvements in social indicators," including infant mortality, life expectancy, educational achievement. But while these and other indicators of human development have been very impressive,[12] he admits this growth in both economic and social indicators came at the price of "political authoritarianism, human rights violations, corruption, union repression, gender discrimination, mistreatment of ethnic minorities, and so on."[13]

NOTES

1   United Nations, "Background," un.org, accessed October 21, 2015, http://www.un.org/millenniumgoals/bkgd.shtml.

2   William Easterly, "How the Millennium Development Goals are Unfair to Africa," Working Paper 14, Brookings Global Economy & Development (November 2007), accessed October 21, 2015, http://www.brookings.edu/~/media/research/files/papers/2007/11/poverty-easterly/11_poverty_easterly.pdf.

3   Charles Gore, "The MDG Paradigm, Productive Capacities, and the Future of Poverty Reduction," *IDS Bulletin* 41, no. 1 (2010): 70.

4   Gore, "The MDG Paradigm," 71.

5   Ha-Joon Chang, *The East Asian Development Experience: The Miracle, the Crisis and the Future* (London: Zed Books, 2006), 114.

6   Sakiko Fukuda-Parr, "Millennium Development Goals: Why They Matter," *Global Governance* 10, no. 4 (2004): 397.

7   Sakiko Fukuda-Parr and David Hulme, "International Norm Dynamics and 'the End of Poverty': Understanding the Millennium Development Goals (MDGs)" (Manchester: Brooks World Poverty Institute, 2009), 4.

8   Sakiko Fukuda-Parr, "Theory and Policy in International Development: Human Development and Capability Approach and the Millennium Development Goals," *International Studies Review* 13, no. 1 (2011): 123.

9   Ha-Joon Chang, *Bad Samaritans: The Myth of Free Trade and the Secret History of Capitalism* (London: Bloomsbury Publishing, 2010), 130.

10 Ha-Joon Chang, "Institutions and Economic Development: Theory, Policy and History," *Journal of Institutional Economics* 7, no. 4 (2011): 477.

11 Ha-Joon Chang, "Hamlet Without the Prince of Denmark," in *Global Governance at Risk*, eds. David Held and Charles Roger (Cambridge: Polity Press, 2013), 132.

12 Chang, "East Asian Development Experience," 109.

13 Chang, "East Asian Development Experience," 109.

MODULE 12
WHERE NEXT?

KEY POINTS

- Human development* is used as a general theoretical focus for many different studies of development.

- The ideas of human development continue to evolve. The next generation of the United Nations Millennium Development Goals,* for example, will focus more on the environment.

- Haq's work changed the way the world saw economic development. It is now widely accepted that economic growth should serve "real people."

Potential

Mahbub ul Haq's *Reflections on Human Development* will continue to be relevant in the field of development studies. The Belgian economist Ingrid Robeyns* found that the capability approach*— and human development—is often used as a "jumping off point" for different studies.[1]

The development academic Sabina Alkire,* for example, used the capability approach (according to which politics and economics should facilitate our ability to decide what we want to do and to be) in a participatory rural survey* to assess small-scale development projects. She compared three case studies—providing women with either small loans to purchase a goat or female-targeted literacy classes—to test if the capability approach would yield different results than those of a simple cost-benefit analysis.*[2]

Commenting on Alkire's study, Robeyns noted that the "female literacy project is a prime example of a project that would no longer

> **❝The basic purpose of development is to enlarge people's choices. ❞**
> Mahbub ul Haq, *Reflections on Human Development*

be funded if it were evaluated only on a traditional cost-benefit basis … as this project has hardly any effects on women's earnings because there is no local market for female employment." The program was beneficial in other ways, however. As well as learning to read, "the women learned that they are equal to men, that they do not need to suffer abuse, and that literate women can solve their own problems."[3]

Hartley Dean,* a professor of social policy at the London School of Economics, applied the capability approach beyond the developing world, to Europe. He assessed European work-welfare policies* "against social justice criteria," concluding that the European Employment Strategy* (EES) was treating human life only in terms of its ability to contribute to the economy (that is, as human capital:* the total stock of skills, knowledge, ability, and so forth of a given population that may be drawn upon to produce value through labor or expertise).[4] "Certainly," he writes, "in the European context it is the notion of human capital that has predominated and that clearly informs the notion of 'employability' at the heart of the EES." Dean's critique points to a distinction between the ideological commitment to "employability as a worker" and "capability as a human." Employability may lead to investment in a person's skills and training that may produce a return. But investing in capabilities would allow individuals to live a life that they have reason to value.[5]

Future Directions

The American economist Jeffrey Sachs* is concerned with incorporating environmental sustainability in the human development approach. For him, the original Millennium Development Goals have "played an important part" in securing progress against poverty, hunger, disease, and other globally relevant social ills. They have also fostered confidence "that globally agreed goals to fight poverty should continue beyond 2015."[6] In September 2015, the United Nations announced its Sustainable Development Goals* (SDGs), which replaced the MDGs. There are 17 SDGs, including goals related to affordable and clean energy, climate change, and a sustainable environment.[7]

Sachs says that since the SDGs are targeted at all countries, they will "have a different feel about them." They are "not what the rich should do for the poor, but what all countries should do for the global well-being of this generation to come."[8] In 2012, before the goals were published, Sachs proposed a number of example goals. These focused on the three "pillars" of the sustainable development* approach: economic development, environmental sustainability, and social inclusion.[9]

One example of this emphasis on sustainability comes in his second goal: "from 2015 to 2030," he proposed, "all nations will adopt economic strategies that increasingly build on sustainable best-practice technologies, appropriate market incentives, and individual responsibilities." This idea emphasizes practices such as low-carbon energy systems, population stabilization through family planning, and burden sharing for environmental costs between high and low income countries.[10] The Sustainable Development Goals, now published, reflect the commitment of countries to ensuring that developmental issues and environmental issues are seen as complementary, rather than necessitating some kind of trade-off.

Summary

Mahbub ul Haq's *Reflections on Human Development* tells the story of how the United Nations *Human Development Reports** came to be and how they were popularized. The first report inspired a revolution in development thinking. "For too long," Haq wrote, "the recurrent question [in development thinking] was, how much is the nation producing? Increasingly, the question now being asked is, how are its people faring?"[11] Haq was the principle architect behind the first six reports. Unlike those who believed in the neoliberal* orthodoxy that informed development at the time when Haq was writing, Haq did not believe that the purpose of development was to increase Gross Domestic Product* (GDP). He believed the goal of development should be one of "enlarging people's choices."[12]

Haq's approach in the first report was notable for its simplicity. He tore down the orthodox assumption of an "automatic link between economic growth and human progress" and widened the definition of "human progress" to mean enabling people to live a life they had reason to value.[13] He built on this core idea to create the Human Development Index* (HDI). This could be used as an alternative to Gross Domestic Product (GDP) in measuring development. Haq's original HDI measured GDP per capita,* life expectancy, and literacy.

These indicators reflect the degree to which a state's citizens have the opportunity to be wealthy, healthy, and to acquire knowledge. Haq's work led, eventually, to the UN's Millennium Development Goals (MDGs): human development goals for the international community. In 2015 a new set of goals were introduced. As with the MDGs, these goals are based on Haq's work and aim to increase human flourishing,* eradicate poverty, and reduce the impact of climate change.

NOTES

1 Ingrid Robeyns, "The Capability Approach in Practice," *The Journal of Political Philosophy* 14, no. 3 (2006): 353.

2 Sabina Alkire, *Valuing Freedoms: Sen's Capability Approach and Poverty Reduction* (Oxford: Oxford University Press, 2002), 235, 256.

3 Robeyns, "The Capability Approach in Practice," 362.

4   Hartley Dean et al., "Developing Capabilities and Rights in Welfare-to-Work Policies," *European Societies* 7, no. 1 (2005): 4.

5   Dean, "Developing Capabilities," 9.

6   Jeffrey D. Sachs, "From Millennium Development Goals to Sustainable Development Goals," *The Lancet* 379, no. 9832 (2012): 2206.

7   United Nations, "The Global Goals," accessed October 22, 2015, http://www.globalgoals.org.

8   Sachs, "Millennium Development Goals," 2208.

9   Sachs, "Millennium Development Goals," 2208.

10 Sachs, "Millennium Development Goals," 2208.

11 Mahbub ul Haq, *Reflections on Human Development* (Oxford: Oxford University Press, 1995), 25.

12 Haq, *Reflections*, 14–5.

13 Haq, *Reflections*, 21.

GLOSSARY

GLOSSARY OF TERMS

20:20 compact: a framework for development cooperation that proposes to reorient existing budgets to human development matters: 20 percent of foreign aid from developed countries and 20 percent of a developing country's budget should be earmarked for social concerns.

Adjustment: Structural Adjustment Programs (SAPs) engage in adjustment, which involves changing economic policies/conditions in order to improve economic outcomes.

Arithmetic mean: the "simple mean," an average calculated by adding each number in a set and dividing it by the total number of numbers.

Austrian school of economics: a family of economic theories originating in Austria in the late-nineteenth century. Austrian economists tend to believe the economy cannot be administered centrally and focus on the economy as the aggregate of individual decisions, avoiding analysis of structural factors.

Basic needs approach: an approach to development that emphasizes the identification and fulfillment of basic needs, such as food, shelter, and physical safety.

Bretton Woods Institutions (International Monetary Fund and World Bank): monetary management institutions, founded at an international conference at the Bretton Woods resort in the US in 1944. Nominally run by many states, they have historically been influenced by American interests in spreading free-market capitalism.

Capability approach: a political philosophy emphasizing that the aim of politics and economics should be to increase human capabilities (what people decide rationally they want to be able to do and to be).

Capitalism: an economic system that focuses on private property rights, and the pursuit of profit from capital (invested money).

Cold War (1947–91): a period of tension between the United States and the Soviet Union between the end of World War II and the collapse of European communism in 1991. While the two blocs never engaged in direct military conflict, they engaged in covert and proxy wars (sponsoring different sides in a conflict instead of engaging with each other overtly) and espionage against one another.

Cost-benefit analysis: a method of evaluation that adds up all the benefits of a given program, and subtracts the costs.

Development economics: deals with understanding and improving the situation of low-income countries.

***Doi moi*:** the name given to a number of reforms introduced in 1986 in Vietnam to transform the socialist economic system (which disallowed such things as private ownership) into a free-market system.

East Asian model: a development paradigm where a government invests heavily in industrialization in order to build its private sector rapidly.

Equity: equality in the distribution of a nation's wealth.

European Employment Strategy: an agreement between countries of the European Union to coordinate their training, employment regulations, welfare, and related programs.

Gender-related Development Index: a way of calculating the Human Development Index that imposes significant penalties for gender gaps in attainment of wealth, health, and literacy on the main index.

Geometric Mean: a form of average calculated by the nth root of the product of n numbers. That means each number is multiplied together, and the nth root (where n is the number of numbers) is taken of the product. This average does not assume each number is independent of the other numbers in the set (e.g. rates of return from year to year depend on one another).

Global governance: the movement toward integration of individual states into intergovernmental or supranational bodies that negotiate and coordinate policy.

Gross Domestic Product (GDP): the market value of all goods and services produced within a given state in a year. GDP is the traditional indicator used to measure a state's economy.

Gross National Income (GNI): the total value of foreign and domestic production claimed by residents of a country; GNI consists of the Gross Domestic Product plus income earned by foreign residents, minus income earned by domestic non-residents.

Gross National Product (GNP): the market value of all goods and services produced in one year by the residents of a country. It is distinguished from Gross Domestic Product (GDP) by its allocation of production based on ownership of the productive factors and nationality of the labor rather than location of the production.

Human capital: the total stock of competencies, knowledge, and attributes a person has that can be used in the performance of labor and generation of economic value.

Human development: the notion that the creation of wealth and industry in developing countries should focus on enriching the worst off in order to make their lives better, rather than merely raising GDP.

Human Development and Capability Association: a community of academics and practitioners seeking to promote mainstream human development concerns; publishes the *Journal of Human Development and Capabilities*.

Human Development Index (HDI): a composite index that shows a country's overall state of "human development" by presenting life expectancy, education, and wealth as a single number.

Human Development Report: an annual report commissioned by the United Nations Development Program. The report, which is written by a team of leading scholars, economists, and statespeople, assesses a wide range of human development indicators.

Human flourishing: a state of affairs where a person or people is happy and prosperous, living a life he or she has reason to value.

Human Poverty Index (HPI): an indication of the standard of living (focusing on deprivation) in a country used by the *Human Development Reports* from 1997 to 2010, when it was replaced with the Multidimensional Poverty Index (MPI).

Human security: a people-centered approach to security; the term human security expands traditional conceptions of security beyond a state's military-territorial concerns to the concerns of individuals, placing issues such as water cleanliness on a par with national security.

Industrialization: the process by which a country or region adopts a primarily industrial economy, at the expense of a primarily agricultural economy.

Informal employment: working in casual sectors without job security, such as doing odd jobs or collecting rubbish to sell on; it is not taxed, protected, or monitored by the government.

International Monetary Fund (IMF): a Washington-based international financial organization founded in 1944. Through its loans to countries, it fosters monetary cooperation, financial stability, high employment, and economic growth.

International Norm Dynamics: an international relations theory, proposed by academics Martha Finnemore and Kathryn Sikkink, where a "norm" (an idea about correct behavior) emerges, cascades through groups that persuade others to adopt it, and eventually becomes internalized (assimilated) into mainstream society. Human rights, for example, started as an idea about the inherent dignity of humans, was promoted by states such as the US and institutions such as the United Nations, and has now become internalized in many other states.

Keynesian economics: an economic perspective advocating that governments ought to promote full employment during recessions by increasing spending in the short run.

Liberalism: a political philosophy that emphasizes individual choice and freedom.

Logarithm: the opposite of an exponent. The simple logarithm (which assumes a base of 10) of 1000 is 3, as 10 must be multiplied by itself three times (10 x 10 x 10) to produce 1000.

Mahbub ul Haq Human Development Center: a think tank (a body of people with specialist knowledge proposing and arguing for certain kinds of policy) in Islamabad, Pakistan, set up by Haq in 1995 in order to promote human development in South Asia.

Millennium Development Goals: eight international development goals set by the United Nations in 2000 to be achieved by 2015. They were to eradicate poverty and hunger, to achieve universal primary education, to promote gender equality, to reduce child mortality, to improve maternal health, to combat disease, to ensure environmental sustainability, and to develop a global partnership for development. Each of the eight goals had a number of quantifiable sub-goals, such as halving the proportion of people living on less than $1.25 USD per day.

Neoliberalism: a political and economic approach that emphasizes the power of free markets to prompt development; neoliberalism supports free trade, deregulation, open markets, and private (as opposed to state) ownership. In the 1980s, it was used as a pejorative term to describe radically pro-market reform.

North-South Roundtable: a forum for development policy cooperation between donor and recipient states founded in 1977.

Official Development Assistance (ODA): the sum of money set aside by a government to transfer to the developing world, either directly or through institutions such as the World Bank or European Union.

Organization for Economic Cooperation and Development (OECD): an international economic organization of 34 of the most developed countries; its aim is to stimulate broad economic progress and trade.

Participatory Rural Survey: a social science data collection methodology according to which the researcher goes into rural communities and asks them to appraise their own development status and communicate it in their own preferred way.

Partition of India: the separation in 1947 of the British Indian empire into multiple independent states: India, West Pakistan (later Pakistan), and East Pakistan (later Bangladesh).

Per capita: a Latin phrase meaning "per head," used to indicate something "per person."

Physical Quality of Life Index (PQLI): developed for the Overseas Development Council in 1975 as an alternative to GDP. It calculates the average of the literacy rate, the infant mortality rate, and life expectancy.

Political economy: an academic discipline that examines the intersection of market factors and non-market factors, especially political activity (governments responding to political pressure to raise or lower taxes, for example).

Political Freedom Index: an index proposed in early *Human Development Reports* to measure the "freedom" of certain countries by analyzing four qualitative factors: political participation, freedom of expression, rule of law, and nondiscrimination. Now, a stand-alone Political Freedom Index is published by Freedom House (an independent watchdog organization founded in 1941 in the US), based on a checklist comprising different dimensions of political rights and civil liberties.

Poverty reduction: a philosophy in development economics that emphasizes the role of development in lifting people out of poverty, rather than building the economy (it sees growth and poverty reduction as related, but distinct, activities).

Satva: a concept in Hindu philosophy equivalent to perfection; for an object or human to have *satva*, it must be completely purified of evil and spread only goodness.

Soviet Union (1922–91): a superstate encompassing most of the communist countries in Central Asia, with Moscow as its capital. The state dissolved after the Cold War ended.

Structural Adjustment Programs (SAPs): reform packages given to developing countries by the International Monetary Fund and World Bank as conditions on loans. SAPs are meant to make these countries more market oriented.

Supranational: a term to describe an organization that has power over national governments or that transcends national borders.

Sustainable development: development that is concerned, to a significant degree, with ensuring that economic enrichment is done in an environmentally friendly way.

Sustainable Development Goals: the 17 UN-backed targets proposed in 2015 that build on and follow from the Millennium Development Goals. They are broader in scope than the MDGs, and focus more directly on mitigating the impact of development on the environment (as well as increasing standards of living around the world).

Trickle-down economics: the belief that greater wealth gains, even those that are inequitable, will eventually benefit everyone, as the disproportionately wealthy spend and stimulate the economy. This viewpoint, while popular in the 1980s and 1990s, has fallen out of favor in the economics profession, though it remains popular with conservative politicians in the West.

United Nations: an intergovernmental organization founded in 1945 and based in New York City, comprised of nearly every state in the world. Its most important functions include overseeing global security matters and administering and promoting global cooperation.

United Nations Development Fund for Women (UNIFEM): a pool of money established in 1976 and administered by the United Nations that is intended to support programs to empower women in the developing world.

United Nations Development Program (UNDP): an executive board in the United Nations System founded in 1965 and dedicated both to reducing poverty and to a number of broader human development goals including the promotion of global health, literacy, and democracy.

United Nations Security Council: One of the six main organs of the United Nations, with primary responsibility for maintenance of international peace and security. Only the Security Council has the power to make decisions that member states are then obligated to implement under the UN Charter.

Washington Consensus: the term given to 10 policy themes recommended and imposed on developing countries in the form of loan conditions by Washington-based financial institutions and promoted by the American government. The policies emphasize macroeconomic (that is, the economy as a whole) stabilization, economic liberalization, and deficit reduction.

Work-welfare policies: policies that connect the reception of state aid to the reentry of the recipient into the labor market.

World Bank: a Washington-based international financial institution founded in 1944 that provides loans to low-income countries. Its decisions are guided by a commitment to facilitating foreign investment and promoting trade integration.

World War II (1939–45): a global war between the vast majority of states, including all great powers of the time, involving over 100 million people from all continents, with the primary theaters of war in the Pacific and Europe. It was fought between the Axis powers (Germany, Italy, Japan) and the Allies (initially France and the United Kingdom, expanding to include Soviet Russia and the US). The Allies achieved victory in Europe on May 8, 1945, and in the Pacific later that year on August 8.

PEOPLE MENTIONED IN THE TEXT

Sabina Alkire is a development academic currently working at the University of Oxford, directing the Oxford Poverty and Human Development Initiative research center.

Aristotle (384–322 B.C.E.) was a Greek philosopher who wrote on a wide range of topics, best known for his thoughts on economics, politics, and ethics. His writing established the basis of Western philosophy.

Ha-Joon Chang (b. 1963) is a Korean economist currently serving as the head of the development department at the University of Cambridge in the UK. In addition to acting as a consultant to the United Nations and the World Bank (among other institutions), he has famously argued that the free-market and free-trade institutions promoted by Western interests "kick away the ladder" toward government-led industrialization.

Martha Chen (b. 1944) is a lecturer in public policy at the Harvard Kennedy School and an affiliated professor at the Harvard Graduate School of Design, both in the US. She works extensively with the UN and other international development organizations, especially focusing on South Asia.

Hartley Dean (b. 1949) is a professor of social policy at the London School of Economics and co-edits the *Journal of Social Policy*. He is interested in understanding the rights of citizens of developing countries.

William H. Draper III (b. 1928) is an American venture capitalist and international statesman. He served as head of the United Nations Development Program between 1986 and 1993.

William Easterly (b. 1957) is an American economist specializing in growth and foreign aid. He is a prominent critic of aid strategies, and believes that seemingly philanthropic programs are actually imperialism in another form.

Martha Finnemore (b. 1959) is an American international relations academic in the constructivist tradition: she examines how ideas and norms are agreed upon by international actors (people operating at an international level) and influence behavior.

Sakiko Fukuda-Parr (b. 1950) is a Japanese academic and international statesperson currently living in the United States. She has acted as an advisor and director in the United Nations Development Program (1979–94), and was Director of the Human Development Report Office between 1995 and 2004.

Charles Gore is a development academic currently teaching at the University of Glasgow. He was a member of the UN Experts Group on the UN Millennium Project (formulating the Millennium Development Goals).

Friedrich Hayek (1899–1992) was an Austrian British economist who famously defended individual liberty and free markets as the only way to organize a just society.

David Hulme (b. 1952) is an English development economist at the University of Manchester, and also director of the Brooks World Poverty Institute. His popular book *Just Give Money to the Poor* (2010) suggests that development aid, rather than supporting administrative apparatus, should flow to households so they can lift themselves out of poverty.

Richard Jolly (b. 1934) is a British statesman and development academic at the University of Sussex. He has held many positions at the UN, most notably as assistant secretary-general (1982–2000), and in 1996 was appointed coordinator of the *Human Development Report*.

Immanuel Kant (1724–1804) was a German philosopher best known for his defense of the idea that all people were worthy of equal consideration and respect, based on the notion that one should act as though one's actions were the universal law (the "categorical imperative").

John Maynard Keynes (1883–1946) was a British economist, most famous for his *General Theory of Employment, Interest, and Money.* This work famously argued that state interventions can moderate the effect of business cycles.

Michael Kevane is an American professor of economics at Santa Clara University. He is interested in the effects on development of increased access to education.

Jacques de Larosière (b. 1929) is a French statesman and has been a prominent member of many international institutions. He was managing director of the International Monetary Fund (IMF) (1978–87), and president of the European Bank for Reconstruction and Development (1993–8).

Ratan Lal Basu (b. 1948) is an Indian economist and science fiction author. He is primarily interested in the contribution of ancient Indian philosophy to modern economic thought.

Mark McGillivray is an Australian professor of international development at Deakin University in Australia. He has worked at the

Australian Agency for International Development, and written
extensively on the allocation of aid and the effectiveness of measuring
human well-being.

Adil Najam is a Pakistani academic who works in America and
Pakistan. He has been on the United Nations Committee for
Development Policy since 2008, working closely on issues of
development and climate change.

Jan Nederveen Pieterse (b. 1946) is a Dutch global studies
academic currently working at the University of California, Santa
Barbara. He is concerned with exploring the relationship between
international development and Western imperialism.

Martha Nussbaum (b. 1947) is an American philosopher and
academic at the University of Chicago. She is notable for her interest
in the revival of ancient Greek philosophy and the applicability of
Aristotelian principals to modern development economics.

Gustav Ranis (1924–2013) was a professor of development at Yale
University.

Martin Ravallion (b. 1952) is an Australian professor of
development economics currently working at Georgetown University
in Washington, US. He is primarily concerned with creating strategies
for poverty reduction.

Debraj Ray (b. 1957) is an Indian American economist and
professor of economics at New York University.

Ingrid Robeyns (b. 1972) is a Belgian economist and development
academic. She holds the chair of ethics of institutions at Utrecht

University, the Netherlands and the chair of the chamber ethics/ practical philosophy at the Dutch Research School of Philosophy.

Jeffrey Sachs (b. 1954) is an American economist and professor. At 28 he was the youngest economics professor in the history of Harvard University, and between 2002 and 2006 he served as director of the United Nations Millennium Project, which formulated the Millennium Development Goals and monitored their implementation.

Ambuj Sagar is an Indian associate at the Belfer Center for Science and International Affairs at Harvard University and a professor of policy studies at the Indian Institute of Technology Delhi. He was a staff researcher at the White House and advises the Indian government on development and climate change.

Amartya Sen (b. 1933) is an Indian economist and Nobel laureate (awarded the Nobel Prize in Economics in 1998 for his work on welfare economics). He is a professor at Harvard University and a fellow at the universities of Cambridge and Oxford.

A. K. Shiva Kumar (b. 1956) is an Indian development economist and academic—he is based in both the US (at Harvard) and in India (at the Indian School of Business). He is a regular contributor to the *Human Development Report*.

Kathryn Sikkink (b. 1955) is an American international relations academic in the constructivist tradition and a professor at Harvard University.

Adam Smith (1723–90) was a Scottish political philosopher widely considered to be the founding father of the discipline of economics with his book *The Wealth of Nations*.

Thirukodikaval Nilakanta Srinivasan (b. 1933) is an Indian economist and professor at Yale University. He was a special adviser at the World Bank (1977–80).

Frances Stewart (b.1940) is a British development economist and professor emeritus of development economics at the University of Oxford. She worked with Haq and his team on the first *Human Development Reports*.

Paul Streeten (b. 1917) is an Austrian development academic who works in Britain and America. He was a major proponent of the basic needs approach and served on the editorial board of the *Human Development Report*.

John Williamson (b. 1937) is an English economist and international statesman famous for coining the term "Washington Consensus" to describe the pro-free-market policy mix promoted by international financial institutions in the 1980s. He has worked with the United Nations, World Bank, and International Monetary Fund in advisory capacities.

WORKS CITED

WORKS CITED

Alkire, Sabina. *Valuing Freedoms: Sen's Capability Approach and Poverty Reduction*. Oxford: Oxford University Press, 2002.

Aristotle. *Nicomachean Ethics*. Translated by C. D. C. Reeve. Indianapolis: Hackett, 2014.

The Politics and the Constitution of Athens. Edited by Stephen Everson. Cambridge: Cambridge University Press, 1996.

Baru, Sanjaya. "Mahbub ul Haq and Human Development: A Tribute." *Economic and Political Weekly* 33, no. 35 (1998): 2275–9.

Chang, Ha-Joon. *The East Asian Development Experience: The Miracle, the Crisis and the Future*. London: Zed Books, 2006.

"Hamlet Without the Prince of Denmark." In *Global Governance at Risk*, edited by David Held and Charles Roger, 129–49. Cambridge: Polity Press, 2013.

Bad Samaritans: The Myth of Free Trade and the Secret History of Capitalism. London: Bloomsbury Publishing, 2010.

"Institutions and Economic Development: Theory, Policy, and History." *Journal of Institutional Economics* 7, no. 4 (2011): 473–89.

Chen, Martha, Joann Vanek, Francine Lund, James Heintz, Renana Jhabvala, and Christine Bonner. *Progress of the World's Women 2005*. New York: United Nations Development Fund For Women, 2005.

Dean, Hartley, Jean-Michel Bonvin, Pascale Vielle, and Nicolas Farvaque. "Developing Capabilities and Rights in Welfare-to-Work Policies." *European Societies* 7, no. 1 (2005): 3–26.

Easterly, William. "How the Millennium Development Goals are Unfair to Africa." Working Paper 14, Brookings Global Economy & Development (November 2007). Accessed October 21, 2015. http://www.brookings.edu/~/media/research/files/papers/2007/11/poverty-easterly/11_poverty_easterly.pdf.

Fukuda-Parr, Sakiko. "The Human Development Paradigm: Operationalizing Sen's Ideas on Capabilities." *Feminist Economics* 9, nos. 2–3 (2003): 301–17.

"The Intellectual Journey Continues." In *Pioneering the Human Development Revolution: An Intellectual Biography of Mahbub ul Haq*, edited by Khadija Haq and Richard Ponzio, 223–55. Oxford: Oxford University Press, 2008.

"Millennium Development Goals: Why They Matter." *Global Governance* 10, no. 4 (2004): 395–402.

"Theory and Policy in International Development: Human Development and Capability Approach and the Millennium Development Goals." *International Studies Review* 13, no. 1 (2011): 122–32.

"What Does Feminization of Poverty Mean? It Isn't Just Lack of Income." *Feminist Economics* 5, no. 2 (1999): 99–103.

Fukuda-Parr, Sakiko and David Hulme. "International Norm Dynamics and 'the End of Poverty:' Understanding the Millennium Development Goals (MDGs)." Manchester: Brooks World Poverty Institute, 2009.

Fukuda-Parr, Sakiko, and A. K. Shiva Kumar, eds. *Readings in Human Development*. New Delhi: Oxford University Press India, 2003.

Gore, Charles. "The MDG Paradigm, Productive Capacities, and the Future of Poverty Reduction." *IDS Bulletin* 41, no. 1 (2010): 70–79.

Grant, James P. *UNICEF Annual Report 1987*. New York: United Nations, 1987. Accessed October 21, 2015. http://www.unicef.org/about/history/files/unicef_annual_report_1987.pdf.

Haq, Mahbub ul. *Reflections on Human Development*. Oxford: Oxford University Press, 1995.

Reflections on Human Development. New Delhi: Oxford University Press India, 1999.

The Poverty Curtain: Choices for the Third World. New York: Columbia University Press, 1976.

The Strategy of Economic Planning. Oxford: Oxford University Press, 1963.

Haq, Mahbub ul, Richard Jolly, Paul Streeten, and Khadija Haq. *The UN and the Bretton Woods Institutions: New Challenges for the Twenty-First Century.* New York: Macmillan, 1995.

Hayek, F. A. *The Road to Serfdom: Texts and Documents – The Definitive Edition*. Edited by Bruce Caldwell. Chicago: Chicago University Press, 2008.

Jillani, M. S., and Masooda Bano. "From Growth to 'Growth With A Social Conscience.'" In *Pioneering the Human Development Revolution: An Intellectual Biography of Mahbub ul Haq*, edited by Khadija Haq and Richard Ponzio, 18–41. Oxford: Oxford University Press, 2008.

Jolly, Richard. "Human Development and Neoliberalism: Paradigms Compared." In *Readings in Human Development*, edited by Sakiko Fukuda-Parr and A. K. Shiva Kumar, 106–17. New Delhi: Oxford University Press India, 2003.

Jolly, Richard, Louis Emmerij, and Thomas Weiss. *UN Ideas that Changed the World*. Indianapolis: Indiana University Press, 2009.

Kant, Immanuel. *Groundwork for the Metaphysics of Morals*, translated by Allen W. Wood. New Haven: Yale University Press, 2002.

Kevane, Michael. "*Reflections on Human Development* by Mahbub ul Haq." *Journal of Economic Literature* 35, no. 1 (1997): 177–8.

Keynes, John Maynard. *The General Theory of Employment, Interest, and Money.* London: Macmillan, 1954.

Lal Basu, Ratan. "Why the Human Development Index Does Not Live Up to Ancient Indian Standards." *Culture Mandala* 6, no. 2 (2005): 1–7.

McGillivray, Mark. "The Human Development Index: Yet Another Redundant Composite Indicator?" *World Development* 19, no. 10 (1991): 1461–8.

Nederveen Pieterse, Jan. "The *Human Development Report* and Cultural Liberty: Tough Liberalism." *Development and Change* 36, no. 6 (2005): 1267–73.

Nussbaum, Martha. "Non-Relative Virtues: An Aristotelian Approach." *Midwest Studies of Philosophy* 13, no. 1 (1988): 32–53.

Organization of Economic Cooperation and Development. *Shaping the 21st Century: The Contribution of Development Cooperation.* Paris: OECD, 1996.

Ranis, Gustav, and Frances Stewart. "Successful Transition Towards a Virtuous Cycle of Human Development and Economic Growth: Country Studies." Economic Growth Center, Yale University (2006). Accessed October 21, 2015. http://www.econ.yale.edu/growth_pdf/cdp943.pdf.

Ravallion, Martin. "Troubling Trade-offs in the Human Development Index." *Journal of Development Economics* 99, no. 2 (2012): 201–9.

Ray, Debraj. *Development Economics*. Princeton: Princeton University Press, 1998.

Robeyns, Ingrid. "The Capability Approach in Practice." *The Journal of Practical Philosophy* 14, no. 3 (2006): 351–76.

Sachs, Jeffrey. "From Millennium Development Goals to Sustainable Development Goals." *The Lancet* 379, no. 9832 (2012): 2206–11.

Sagar, Ambuj D., and Adil Najam. "The Human Development Index: A Critical Review." *Ecological Economics* 25, no. 3 (1998): 249–64.

Sen, Amartya. "A Decade of Human Development." *Journal of Human Development* 1, no. 1 (2000): 17–23.

"Development as Capability Expansion." In *Readings in Human Development*, edited by Sakiko Fukuda-Parr and A. K. Shiva Kumar, 3–17. New Delhi: Oxford University Press India, 2003.

Development as Freedom. Oxford: Oxford University Press, 1999.

"Foreword." In *Readings in Human Development*, edited by Sakiko Fukuda-Parr and A. K. Shiva Kumar, vii-xiii. New Delhi: Oxford University Press India, 2003.

Sen, Amartya, and Tam Dalyell. "Obituary: Mahbub ul Haq." *Independent* (1998). Accessed October 21, 2015. http://www.independent.co.uk/arts-entertainment/obituary-mahbub-ul Haq-1169323.html.

Smith, Adam. *An Enquiry into the Nature and Causes of the Wealth of Nations.* New York: Random House, 1937.

Srinivasan, T. N. "Human Development: A New Paradigm or Reinvention of the Wheel?" *The American Economic Review* 84, no. 2 (1994): 238–43.

Streeten, Paul. *First Things First: Meeting Basic Human Needs in Developing Countries*. World Bank, 1981.

United Nations. "Background." Accessed October 21, 2015. http://www.un.org/millenniumgoals/bkgd.shtml.

"The Global Goals." Accessed September 11, 2015. http://www.globalgoals.org.

United Nations Development Program. "About the Reports." Human Development Reports. Accessed March 6, 2014. http://hdr.undp.org/en/content/about-reports.

"Human Development Index (HDI)." Human Development Reports. Accessed October 22, 2015. http://hdr.undp.org/en/statistics/hdi.

Human Development Report 1990. New York: Oxford University Press, 1990.

Human Development Report 1991. New York: Oxford University Press, 1991.

Human Development Report 1994. New York: Oxford University Press, 1994.

Human Development Report 1995. New York: Oxford University Press, 1995.

Human Development Report 1997. New York: Oxford University Press, 1997.

Human Development Report 2000. New York: Oxford University Press, 2000.

Human Development Report 2004: Cultural Liberty in Today's Diverse World. New York: Oxford University Press, 2004.

Social Services for Human Development: Vietnam Human Development Report 2011. Hanoi: United Nations, 2011.

Williamson, John. *Latin American Adjustment: How Much Has Happened?* Accessed March 1, 2014. Peterson Institute of International Economics, 1990, Chapter 2. http://www.iie.com/publications/papers/paper.cfm?researchid=486.

THE MACAT LIBRARY
BY DISCIPLINE

AFRICANA STUDIES

Chinua Achebe's *An Image of Africa: Racism in Conrad's Heart of Darkness*
W. E. B. Du Bois's *The Souls of Black Folk*
Zora Neale Huston's *Characteristics of Negro Expression*
Martin Luther King Jr's *Why We Can't Wait*
Toni Morrison's *Playing in the Dark: Whiteness in the American Literary Imagination*

ANTHROPOLOGY

Arjun Appadurai's *Modernity at Large: Cultural Dimensions of Globalisation*
Philippe Ariès's *Centuries of Childhood*
Franz Boas's *Race, Language and Culture*
Kim Chan & Renée Mauborgne's *Blue Ocean Strategy*
Jared Diamond's *Guns, Germs & Steel: the Fate of Human Societies*
Jared Diamond's *Collapse: How Societies Choose to Fail or Survive*
E. E. Evans-Pritchard's *Witchcraft, Oracles and Magic Among the Azande*
James Ferguson's *The Anti-Politics Machine*
Clifford Geertz's *The Interpretation of Cultures*
David Graeber's *Debt: the First 5000 Years*
Karen Ho's *Liquidated: An Ethnography of Wall Street*
Geert Hofstede's *Culture's Consequences: Comparing Values, Behaviors, Institutes and Organizations across Nations*
Claude Lévi-Strauss's *Structural Anthropology*
Jay Macleod's *Ain't No Makin' It: Aspirations and Attainment in a Low-Income Neighborhood*
Saba Mahmood's *The Politics of Piety: The Islamic Revival and the Feminist Subject*
Marcel Mauss's *The Gift*

BUSINESS

Jean Lave & Etienne Wenger's *Situated Learning*
Theodore Levitt's *Marketing Myopia*
Burton G. Malkiel's *A Random Walk Down Wall Street*
Douglas McGregor's *The Human Side of Enterprise*
Michael Porter's *Competitive Strategy: Creating and Sustaining Superior Performance*
John Kotter's *Leading Change*
C. K. Prahalad & Gary Hamel's *The Core Competence of the Corporation*

CRIMINOLOGY

Michelle Alexander's *The New Jim Crow: Mass Incarceration in the Age of Colorblindness*
Michael R. Gottfredson & Travis Hirschi's *A General Theory of Crime*
Richard Herrnstein & Charles A. Murray's *The Bell Curve: Intelligence and Class Structure in American Life*
Elizabeth Loftus's *Eyewitness Testimony*
Jay Macleod's *Ain't No Makin' It: Aspirations and Attainment in a Low-Income Neighborhood*
Philip Zimbardo's *The Lucifer Effect*

ECONOMICS

Janet Abu-Lughod's *Before European Hegemony*
Ha-Joon Chang's *Kicking Away the Ladder*
David Brion Davis's *The Problem of Slavery in the Age of Revolution*
Milton Friedman's *The Role of Monetary Policy*
Milton Friedman's *Capitalism and Freedom*
David Graeber's *Debt: the First 5000 Years*
Friedrich Hayek's *The Road to Serfdom*
Karen Ho's *Liquidated: An Ethnography of Wall Street*

John Maynard Keynes's *The General Theory of Employment, Interest and Money*
Charles P. Kindleberger's *Manias, Panics and Crashes*
Robert Lucas's *Why Doesn't Capital Flow from Rich to Poor Countries?*
Burton G. Malkiel's *A Random Walk Down Wall Street*
Thomas Robert Malthus's *An Essay on the Principle of Population*
Karl Marx's *Capital*
Thomas Piketty's *Capital in the Twenty-First Century*
Amartya Sen's *Development as Freedom*
Adam Smith's *The Wealth of Nations*
Nassim Nicholas Taleb's *The Black Swan: The Impact of the Highly Improbable*
Amos Tversky's & Daniel Kahneman's *Judgment under Uncertainty: Heuristics and Biases*
Mahbub Ul Haq's *Reflections on Human Development*
Max Weber's *The Protestant Ethic and the Spirit of Capitalism*

FEMINISM AND GENDER STUDIES

Judith Butler's *Gender Trouble*
Simone De Beauvoir's *The Second Sex*
Michel Foucault's *History of Sexuality*
Betty Friedan's *The Feminine Mystique*
Saba Mahmood's *The Politics of Piety: The Islamic Revival and the Feminist Subject*
Joan Wallach Scott's *Gender and the Politics of History*
Mary Wollstonecraft's *A Vindication of the Rights of Women*
Virginia Woolf's *A Room of One's Own*

GEOGRAPHY

The Brundtland Report's *Our Common Future*
Rachel Carson's *Silent Spring*
Charles Darwin's *On the Origin of Species*
James Ferguson's *The Anti-Politics Machine*
Jane Jacobs's *The Death and Life of Great American Cities*
James Lovelock's *Gaia: A New Look at Life on Earth*
Amartya Sen's *Development as Freedom*
Mathis Wackernagel & William Rees's *Our Ecological Footprint*

HISTORY

Janet Abu-Lughod's *Before European Hegemony*
Benedict Anderson's *Imagined Communities*
Bernard Bailyn's *The Ideological Origins of the American Revolution*
Hanna Batatu's *The Old Social Classes And The Revolutionary Movements Of Iraq*
Christopher Browning's *Ordinary Men: Reserve Police Batallion 101 and the Final Solution in Poland*
Edmund Burke's *Reflections on the Revolution in France*
William Cronon's *Nature's Metropolis: Chicago And The Great West*
Alfred W. Crosby's *The Columbian Exchange*
Hamid Dabashi's *Iran: A People Interrupted*
David Brion Davis's *The Problem of Slavery in the Age of Revolution*
Nathalie Zemon Davis's *The Return of Martin Guerre*
Jared Diamond's *Guns, Germs & Steel: the Fate of Human Societies*
Frank Dikotter's *Mao's Great Famine*
John W Dower's *War Without Mercy: Race And Power In The Pacific War*
W. E. B. Du Bois's *The Souls of Black Folk*
Richard J. Evans's *In Defence of History*
Lucien Febvre's *The Problem of Unbelief in the 16th Century*
Sheila Fitzpatrick's *Everyday Stalinism*

The Macat Library By Discipline

LITERATURE

Chinua Achebe's *An Image of Africa: Racism in Conrad's Heart of Darkness*
Roland Barthes's *Mythologies*
Homi K. Bhabha's *The Location of Culture*
Judith Butler's *Gender Trouble*
Simone De Beauvoir's *The Second Sex*
Ferdinand De Saussure's *Course in General Linguistics*
T. S. Eliot's *The Sacred Wood: Essays on Poetry and Criticism*
Zora Neale Huston's *Characteristics of Negro Expression*
Toni Morrison's *Playing in the Dark: Whiteness in the American Literary Imagination*
Edward Said's *Orientalism*
Gayatri Chakravorty Spivak's *Can the Subaltern Speak?*
Mary Wollstonecraft's *A Vindication of the Rights of Women*
Virginia Woolf's *A Room of One's Own*

PHILOSOPHY

Elizabeth Anscombe's *Modern Moral Philosophy*
Hannah Arendt's *The Human Condition*
Aristotle's *Metaphysics*
Aristotle's *Nicomachean Ethics*
Edmund Gettier's *Is Justified True Belief Knowledge?*
Georg Wilhelm Friedrich Hegel's *Phenomenology of Spirit*
David Hume's *Dialogues Concerning Natural Religion*
David Hume's *The Enquiry for Human Understanding*
Immanuel Kant's *Religion within the Boundaries of Mere Reason*
Immanuel Kant's *Critique of Pure Reason*
Søren Kierkegaard's *The Sickness Unto Death*
Søren Kierkegaard's *Fear and Trembling*
C. S. Lewis's *The Abolition of Man*
Alasdair MacIntyre's *After Virtue*
Marcus Aurelius's *Meditations*
Friedrich Nietzsche's *On the Genealogy of Morality*
Friedrich Nietzsche's *Beyond Good and Evil*
Plato's *Republic*
Plato's *Symposium*
Jean-Jacques Rousseau's *The Social Contract*
Gilbert Ryle's *The Concept of Mind*
Baruch Spinoza's *Ethics*
Sun Tzu's *The Art of War*
Ludwig Wittgenstein's *Philosophical Investigations*

POLITICS

Benedict Anderson's *Imagined Communities*
Aristotle's *Politics*
Bernard Bailyn's *The Ideological Origins of the American Revolution*
Edmund Burke's *Reflections on the Revolution in France*
John C. Calhoun's *A Disquisition on Government*
Ha-Joon Chang's *Kicking Away the Ladder*
Hamid Dabashi's *Iran: A People Interrupted*
Hamid Dabashi's *Theology of Discontent: The Ideological Foundation of the Islamic Revolution in Iran*
Robert Dahl's *Democracy and its Critics*
Robert Dahl's *Who Governs?*
David Brion Davis's *The Problem of Slavery in the Age of Revolution*

The Macat Library By Discipline

Alexis De Tocqueville's *Democracy in America*
James Ferguson's *The Anti-Politics Machine*
Frank Dikotter's *Mao's Great Famine*
Sheila Fitzpatrick's *Everyday Stalinism*
Eric Foner's *Reconstruction: America's Unfinished Revolution, 1863-1877*
Milton Friedman's *Capitalism and Freedom*
Francis Fukuyama's *The End of History and the Last Man*
John Lewis Gaddis's *We Now Know: Rethinking Cold War History*
Ernest Gellner's *Nations and Nationalism*
David Graeber's *Debt: the First 5000 Years*
Antonio Gramsci's *The Prison Notebooks*
Alexander Hamilton, John Jay & James Madison's *The Federalist Papers*
Friedrich Hayek's *The Road to Serfdom*
Christopher Hill's *The World Turned Upside Down*
Thomas Hobbes's *Leviathan*
John A. Hobson's *Imperialism: A Study*
Samuel P. Huntington's *The Clash of Civilizations and the Remaking of World Order*
Tony Judt's *Postwar: A History of Europe Since 1945*
David C. Kang's *China Rising: Peace, Power and Order in East Asia*
Paul Kennedy's *The Rise and Fall of Great Powers*
Robert Keohane's *After Hegemony*
Martin Luther King Jr.'s *Why We Can't Wait*
Henry Kissinger's *World Order: Reflections on the Character of Nations and the Course of History*
John Locke's *Two Treatises of Government*
Niccolò Machiavelli's *The Prince*
Thomas Robert Malthus's *An Essay on the Principle of Population*
Mahmood Mamdani's *Citizen and Subject: Contemporary Africa And The Legacy Of Late Colonialism*
Karl Marx's *Capital*
John Stuart Mill's *On Liberty*
John Stuart Mill's *Utilitarianism*
Hans Morgenthau's *Politics Among Nations*
Thomas Paine's *Common Sense*
Thomas Paine's *Rights of Man*
Thomas Piketty's *Capital in the Twenty-First Century*
Robert D. Putnam's *Bowling Alone*
John Rawls's *Theory of Justice*
Jean-Jacques Rousseau's *The Social Contract*
Theda Skocpol's *States and Social Revolutions*
Adam Smith's *The Wealth of Nations*
Sun Tzu's *The Art of War*
Henry David Thoreau's *Civil Disobedience*
Thucydides's *The History of the Peloponnesian War*
Kenneth Waltz's *Theory of International Politics*
Max Weber's *Politics as a Vocation*
Odd Arne Westad's *The Global Cold War: Third World Interventions And The Making Of Our Times*

POSTCOLONIAL STUDIES

Roland Barthes's *Mythologies*
Frantz Fanon's *Black Skin, White Masks*
Homi K. Bhabha's *The Location of Culture*
Gustavo Gutiérrez's *A Theology of Liberation*
Edward Said's *Orientalism*
Gayatri Chakravorty Spivak's *Can the Subaltern Speak?*

PSYCHOLOGY

Gordon Allport's *The Nature of Prejudice*
Alan Baddeley & Graham Hitch's *Aggression: A Social Learning Analysis*
Albert Bandura's *Aggression: A Social Learning Analysis*
Leon Festinger's *A Theory of Cognitive Dissonance*
Sigmund Freud's *The Interpretation of Dreams*
Betty Friedan's *The Feminine Mystique*
Michael R. Gottfredson & Travis Hirschi's *A General Theory of Crime*
Eric Hoffer's *The True Believer: Thoughts on the Nature of Mass Movements*
William James's *Principles of Psychology*
Elizabeth Loftus's *Eyewitness Testimony*
A. H. Maslow's *A Theory of Human Motivation*
Stanley Milgram's *Obedience to Authority*
Steven Pinker's *The Better Angels of Our Nature*
Oliver Sacks's *The Man Who Mistook His Wife For a Hat*
Richard Thaler & Cass Sunstein's *Nudge: Improving Decisions About Health, Wealth and Happiness*
Amos Tversky's *Judgment under Uncertainty: Heuristics and Biases*
Philip Zimbardo's *The Lucifer Effect*

SCIENCE

Rachel Carson's *Silent Spring*
William Cronon's *Nature's Metropolis: Chicago And The Great West*
Alfred W. Crosby's *The Columbian Exchange*
Charles Darwin's *On the Origin of Species*
Richard Dawkin's *The Selfish Gene*
Thomas Kuhn's *The Structure of Scientific Revolutions*
Geoffrey Parker's *Global Crisis: War, Climate Change and Catastrophe in the Seventeenth Century*
Mathis Wackernagel & William Rees's *Our Ecological Footprint*

SOCIOLOGY

Michelle Alexander's *The New Jim Crow: Mass Incarceration in the Age of Colorblindness*
Gordon Allport's *The Nature of Prejudice*
Albert Bandura's *Aggression: A Social Learning Analysis*
Hanna Batatu's *The Old Social Classes And The Revolutionary Movements Of Iraq*
Ha-Joon Chang's *Kicking Away the Ladder*
W. E. B. Du Bois's *The Souls of Black Folk*
Émile Durkheim's *On Suicide*
Frantz Fanon's *Black Skin, White Masks*
Frantz Fanon's *The Wretched of the Earth*
Eric Foner's *Reconstruction: America's Unfinished Revolution, 1863-1877*
Eugene Genovese's *Roll, Jordan, Roll: The World the Slaves Made*
Jack Goldstone's *Revolution and Rebellion in the Early Modern World*
Antonio Gramsci's *The Prison Notebooks*
Richard Herrnstein & Charles A Murray's *The Bell Curve: Intelligence and Class Structure in American Life*
Eric Hoffer's *The True Believer: Thoughts on the Nature of Mass Movements*
Jane Jacobs's *The Death and Life of Great American Cities*
Robert Lucas's *Why Doesn't Capital Flow from Rich to Poor Countries?*
Jay Macleod's *Ain't No Makin' It: Aspirations and Attainment in a Low Income Neighborhood*
Elaine May's *Homeward Bound: American Families in the Cold War Era*
Douglas McGregor's *The Human Side of Enterprise*
C. Wright Mills's *The Sociological Imagination*

Thomas Piketty's *Capital in the Twenty-First Century*
Robert D. Putman's *Bowling Alone*
David Riesman's *The Lonely Crowd: A Study of the Changing American Character*
Edward Said's *Orientalism*
Joan Wallach Scott's *Gender and the Politics of History*
Theda Skocpol's *States and Social Revolutions*
Max Weber's *The Protestant Ethic and the Spirit of Capitalism*

THEOLOGY

Augustine's *Confessions*
Benedict's *Rule of St Benedict*
Gustavo Gutiérrez's *A Theology of Liberation*
Carole Hillenbrand's *The Crusades: Islamic Perspectives*
David Hume's *Dialogues Concerning Natural Religion*
Immanuel Kant's *Religion within the Boundaries of Mere Reason*
Ernst Kantorowicz's *The King's Two Bodies: A Study in Medieval Political Theology*
Søren Kierkegaard's *The Sickness Unto Death*
C. S. Lewis's *The Abolition of Man*
Saba Mahmood's *The Politics of Piety: The Islamic Revival and the Feminist Subject*
Baruch Spinoza's *Ethics*
Keith Thomas's *Religion and the Decline of Magic*

COMING SOON

Chris Argyris's *The Individual and the Organisation*
Seyla Benhabib's *The Rights of Others*
Walter Benjamin's *The Work Of Art in the Age of Mechanical Reproduction*
John Berger's *Ways of Seeing*
Pierre Bourdieu's *Outline of a Theory of Practice*
Mary Douglas's *Purity and Danger*
Roland Dworkin's *Taking Rights Seriously*
James G. March's *Exploration and Exploitation in Organisational Learning*
Ikujiro Nonaka's *A Dynamic Theory of Organizational Knowledge Creation*
Griselda Pollock's *Vision and Difference*
Amartya Sen's *Inequality Re-Examined*
Susan Sontag's *On Photography*
Yasser Tabbaa's *The Transformation of Islamic Art*
Ludwig von Mises's *Theory of Money and Credit*